I had never seen a m̶ _[barcode obscures text]_ After her recovery, she an̶ _____ ̶hosted a "Praise the Lord" party. While attending, I recalled the Biblical account in Luke 10 where ten lepers were healed but only one returned to thank the Lord. They all had a disease that was incurable.

During the winter, people were dying from the flu or pneumonia. Lauren had both followed by a cascade of complications which threatened her life. The situation seemed impossible, but she was healed. And now, she is the one returning to thank the Lord and to encourage others. In that Biblical story, the one who returned was then made completely whole. I believe this will be Lauren's reality as she now lives to make the One who saved her known.

—CHAR-LAY DOUGLAS
Production Assistant, America's Got Talent

God's Got This is the story of Lauren in her struggle to survive a deadly illness, her will to live, the challenges she faced and the obstacles she overcame.

It is the story of her mother, Susan, and her absolute determination, and her relentless drive to save her child, her only child, from almost certain death.

Above all, it is a testament to the importance of faith, the power of prayer and to the glory of God, through whom all things are possible.

—DR. NEVEEN M. HABASHI, MD
Critical Care Physician

Lauren is a miracle! She tells her story of "sickness unto death" and how God's healing power gave her new life physically and spiritually. She has a passion to share what God has done, is doing, and will do to inspire every reader.

This story cannot be told without including how her warrior mother turned to God in faith and prayer, as she stood by her daughter's bedside as Lauren battled for her life.

Lauren is a miracle … she is the evidence! *"To God Be the Glory, Great Things He Has Done."*

—Pastor Nathan L. May

God's Got This is the heart-wrenching and life changing journey of my friend Lauren. Her survival is nothing short of miraculous. God was in the smallest of details. His presence was tangible from her first days in critical care all the way through to her rehabilitation. His hand was evident as He provided caring and praying nursing staff and as He miraculously assembled a team of doctors equipped to save her life. The faithfulness of parents and friends is in itself a miraculous story of enduring love. You cannot hear Lauren's story and dispel the power of prayer.

Each time I see my sweet friend walk across the room or smile with her sparkling blue eyes I can only thank God and declare, "We serve a healing Jesus." Jehovah-Rapha – The Lord who heals.

—Heather H. Lockman

Lauren has been my best friend for fifteen years. She has the best heart of anyone I know and will do anything for anyone. Her willingness to invite you into the painful events of 2014 is evidence of that heart.

While she was lying in the hospital fighting for her life, I selfishly prayed that God wouldn't take her from me. She is such a fighter and a blessing to everyone she meets. She has a way to lift spirits and inspire people to believe in the power of prayer and healing. Her story isn't finished yet. She is a walking miracle and I am a better person because she is in my life.

—SARAH RICE

My life has been forever changed by the opportunity to walk through this dark season with Lauren. Going through this difficult journey with her has left me a better person. I am more aware of life and how best to live it. I now find joy in the small every day events that I once took for granted.

Through this journey, I've seen love, loyalty, respect and encouragement in so many faces and in so many ways. I wish I could put into words just how much my life has been enriched through Lauren and her family. Lauren is a true miracle and I am so thankful that God spared her life so that others can now see His love and patience poured out through her.

Lauren's story will draw you closer to the heart of God and remind you of the value of your own life. She is my inspiration and will certainly become an inspiration to all who hear her gripping story.

—TERESA TURNER

What an honor to be the first one asked to proof read this amazing manuscript. You will feel every emotion as this book takes you deep into Lauren and Susan's journey. Powerful! God is going to use this story. I was humbled and blessed. Kim, this is your best writing yet!

—KAY FLETCHER

This is a powerful story of God's faithfulness. You will be challenged and encouraged to believe the improbable. For every reader, Lauren's story is an authentic demonstration of God's love for us.

His power to physically heal and restore is a reminder that Jesus came to heal our sinful hearts and restore us into a right relationship with our Heavenly Father.

Lauren lives for an audience of One while witnessing to many through the trials placed before her. God is being glorified by her faith in this journey. Her story is a testament to what God can and will do when we surrender control and trust in Him.

—JON AND LEEANN ARROWOOD

From leading an active life to the sudden terror of a critical illness, Lauren shares God's awesome faithfulness. A mother's love and drive to do whatever it took to save her daughter will stir your heart. Every page of this book speaks "God's Got This."

—LINDA M. AUTON

Caren,

Love and God's Blessings,
Lauren S. Smith

GOD'S GOT THIS!
Surviving the Tunnel of Change

LAUREN SUMMEY SMITH
WITH KIM FLETCHER

LIFE COMPASS MEDIA

ISBN: 978-1517211486

This book is dedicated to
my mother, Susan Parker.

You willed me back to life
as God heard and answered
the faithful cries of your heart.
No one could ever ask for
a better mother or friend.

I love you in big ways.
I love you in small ways.
I love you this minute.
I'll love you always.

ACKNOWLEDGEMENTS

Many people contributed to the process of my miraculous story being captured in the form of this book. I want to warmly thank every person who joined me on this journey. I wish it were possible to name each and every one of you.

First I wish to thank my mother, Susan Parker, and my Father, Furman (Lum) Summey, Jr. Your faithful presence and prayers are one of the key reasons I am alive to tell this story. Dad, you were the honorary leader of my therapy team.

I also wish to thank my treasured family and friends for the never-ending outpouring of love, presence, prayers, cards, gifts (including flowers and balloons), food, support and encouragement. You sustained my parents while I was fighting for my life.

I want to specifically thank our friend Wayne Lutz who tirelessly drove my parents almost daily to be by my side and for the wonderful care-giving along the way.

To Sarah Rice, my "bestie," thank you for your enduring friendship, for countless hours spent relieving my caregivers, and for always giving me hope as we cried together and laughed together.

To my dear friend, Heather Lockman. Thank you for all of the times you called to sing over me through some of my roughest times. Your friendship, heart-to-heart talks and Godly words of wisdom sustained me.

Teresa Turner, my "sis," thank you for bringing laughter and joy into this dark season that encouraged me and my family.

Thank you Steve for being like a brother as you sat silently, adding much support and for being my personal courier.

Thank you to Barry and Vicky Lewis for all of the hard work to make the "Praise the Lord" party such a success and for the countless others who supplied the food, drinks and decorations for that event.

Donata, thank you for all of the gifts and delicious food you continue to share to this day. Your constant faithfulness to share Scripture-focused encouragement was a true lifeline to Mom and me.

To my family at Merchants Distributors Incorporated (MDI), I will never forget the special gifts stuffed with surprises, the conference calls that kept me in the loop, the personal fundraisers to assist in my medical care, and for making me your Angel Tree recipient in 2014.

God orchestrated the perfect team of medical specialists who literally saved my life. Thank you for your expertise to all of my care-givers, therapists, nurses and physicians. Your faith in me impacted my life and moved me forward in a positive way.

I want to specifically thank Dr. Neveen M. Habashi for showing up at my bedside against all odds and bringing the wisdom to the table that turned me from death toward life on multiple occasions and for your faith in God as the Great Physician.

I also want to thank her brother, Dr. Nader Habashi of the University of Maryland. His research and expertise in the area of advanced ventilation systems for patients on life support provided key insights which allowed my lungs to heal. I trust that your discoveries will permeate and raise the current standard of care for respiratory dependent individuals world-wide.

I want to extend a special thank you to my book team for making this journey possible.

My mother kept daily journals which became my voice during the weeks when I was silenced by a coma. The details she captured added substance and accuracy to my story.

To my dear co-author, I could go on all day. I am grateful for your amazing writing and story-telling talent, your patience, and for turning the reliving of this story from a potential nightmare to a healing journey. At the end of the day, my co-author has now become my friend. Thank you for investing the months of January, February and March, making this book your highest professional priority and for driving to my home to secretly join me while I was still unable to venture out due to a weakened immune system. Thank you for returning that first phone call which led to my idea becoming an actual book, and for allowing God to use you to give my story shape and clarity.

Thank you, Mercy Hope, for being a key support as you offered your God-given creative abilities to the ultimate interior and cover design for this book.

Thank you to Mom, Kim and Kim's Mom, Kay Fletcher, for patiently proof reading with your great eyes for detail.

A special thanks of honor to Pastors Raymond and Shonda Hollis for confirming the writing of this book and for personally visiting to lay hands on me and pray while believing for my total healing.

I also want to thank Pastor Nathan L. May and his wife, Emile for adopting me and Mom, praying for us and encouraging us with your porch visits and for blessing the manuscript before it went to print.

To everyone from the countless churches, social media connections, and community support, thank you for contributing to my life and my story.

And most importantly, thank you God for using me as a vessel by keeping me alive to tell my story through your eyes. You gave my life back to me. I now surrender it back to you to fulfill my highest destiny. Oh, how great Thou art!

CONTENTS

FOREWORD

In a song which became famous years ago, guitarist Buck Dharma told us not to fear the reaper because death comes to us all.

As physicians we see death every day. In medical school we are taught to forge a sacred bond with our patients, to treat them with dignity and respect and above all to do no harm. Yet we are told not to become too emotionally attached to our patients. I've often wondered about that, because it seemed conflicting, but over time I have come to understand why.

We see death every day, and we grieve over the loss of our patients. Such grief is magnified when we have an emotional bond with our patient. Over time we become desensitized to death and we learn to conceal our sorrow. We struggle every day to do the right thing for our patients. Every day we seem to have to battle the bureaucracy to take care of our patients, and it is daunting. We wonder why we continue to fight an uphill battle. Our job is challenging enough.

I found myself disillusioned and weary of all of this. I wondered if I should leave medicine or find another line of work, since now I was a provider of healthcare, a commodity, like a utility or a service instead of a physician charged with the mission of preserving human life, which is not a commodity but a gift. A fragile, fleeting gift that can slip through your fingers at any time.

Then I met Lauren.

I was working in the intensive care unit during the 2013-2014 flu season. I was rounding on the patients in the unit. I stopped dead in my tracks. There was Lauren, a young woman, lying on the bed barely recognizable as a human being. I was horrified. As I moved in closer, I saw the face of a sleeping princess with golden blond hair perfectly laid out on the pillow amidst a confusing sea of tubes and a barrage of monitors and machinery

Then I met Lauren's mother.

She was distraught over the condition of her daughter. I sensed her anguish. She appeared mentally, physically and emotionally exhausted, yet it was obvious that she was not going to let that interfere with her vigilance and her resolve to save her daughter.

And there we were. The three of us. Sleeping beauty, steel magnolia and me.

Their story is quite remarkable. It is the story of Lauren in her struggle to survive a deadly illness, her will to live, the challenges she faced and the obstacles she overcame.

It is the story of her mother, Susan, and her absolute

determination, and her relentless drive to save her child, her only child, from almost certain death.

Above all, it is a testament to the importance of faith, the power of prayer and to the glory of God, through whom all things are possible.

—Dr. Neveen M. Habashi, MD

WORD FROM THE AUTHOR
Lauren Summey Smith

I am sitting with my co-author for one of our first meetings that will unlock the contents which will become the book you now hold in your hand.

Kim walks into the home of my mother where I am still living. The ravages of my illness left me with a weakened body and an equally weak immune system, so going out is not an option. I am on medically-induced house arrest. Thus, Kim came to meet with me today.

When she walked in, she was quick to share the word that kept coming to her as she drove to our meeting. The word was LEGACY. I almost broke into tears, as I said, *"You won't believe what I just told my mom. I told her that this book feels like part of my legacy."*

That moment confirmed that this project was destined by God as a platform to share my story with many I may never meet face to face.

As we sat over coffee and cookies (compliments of the world's greatest mom – my mom), I told Kim a story about my grandfather. My grandparents were on my mind as I was anxiously awaiting a call that my last living grandparent was gravely ill. In that emotional place of remembrance, I shared how I was exceptionally close to my grandfather. So close that he left me a framed piece of art which holds his picture in uniform and his military medals. I went on to share how that image hangs right as I enter my home – a place I know I will return one day when the strength of my body catches up to the strength I now possess in my spirit.

That is when a revelation captured my heart. The medals framed alongside his photo represent part of his legacy of honor, as he had served our country with pride and selflessness during World War II.

I now sat positioned to "frame" my story into this book with one powerful difference. While my grandfather's legacy lives on in many hearts, that framed piece could only hang in one place. This book, on the other hand, has the power to make its way into many hands and hearts.

Now, when I say I "sat positioned," I mean just that. I only have the ability to walk short distances as my endurance and lungs took a hard hit and are still recovering. While the rehabilitation staff measured and fit me with a custom wheelchair of my own, I chose to let it collect dust in the garage while I sat in my grandfather's wheelchair. Somehow, I almost feel as if the armrests of this chair from which I bring forth this book represent his arms embracing me.

Many who survived war eras like my grandfather came

away wounded, scared and traumatized. While I would not be quick to compare my last year to a war, those who supported me from the sidelines and warred with me are indeed quick to say I went into battle with the odds stacked against me. I faced a formidable enemy. I was wounded over and over again by numerous complications and setbacks. I was blind-sided by the relentless hits against my immune system and my lungs. If medals were given for surviving such an overwhelming assault against ones health, my co-author says I would have my own framed shadow box of medals to commemorate my victories.

There is no shadow box. But there is a book! As a woman without my own biological children, I believe that this book represents a powerful portion of my legacy. I am now sitting here in this chair wondering what lessons I hope to instill in those who will be influenced by my story.

I was blessed to survive … I know that now. But believe me, there were many days where joining Jesus by death would have been easier, much easier. But I did indeed survive and now, while I could be watching TV and eating snacks in a state of depression over my ongoing quarantined season of my recovery, I choose a different path. I am choosing to release the right to keep this story to myself and release it into God's hands for Him to use as He chooses.

For the sake of my legacy and in honor of the One who gave me back my life, I choose:

- faith over hopelessness
- joy over depression

- purpose over pain
- gratitude over bitterness
- destiny over defeat
- victory against all odds

I wish each of you could visit my home and see the shadow box hanging with those medals that were proudly passed along to me. They help me to remember. I trust this book will help you remember that all of life is a gift, even the grueling parts, and that you have more value and purpose than you ever imagined.

You see, I now know more than ever that every day is a gift. I have my life back, even though it is a bit altered from what I might have dreamed. I am hoping that by the spring, I will be strong enough to go outside of this house and begin to live my life again.

I became sick in the winter, missing the spring, summer and fall of 2014. Now winter of 2015, I'm finding time to put my story into print … just in time for spring. Out of the harshness of winter comes the spring. New life is inevitable! It will come. The question is, will we embrace it and steward it well?

Regardless of the season in which you find yourself, I trust that my willingness to share this story and expose my heart on its hardest days will feel like a gift of hope. My prayer for this book is that it will awaken you to the precious fact that life is short and how we spend our days really does matter.

I have been to the brink of death and back to compel you to live your life to the fullest every day. There is one source of life and His name is Jesus.

The fact I survived is only part of the miracle. The fact I get to now share that story with you from a place of gratitude, legacy and destiny is the other part. That is the part that lives on.

So read on and know that if it is true for me, it is also true for you that "God's Got This!"

—Lauren Summey Smith

WORD FROM THE AUTHOR
Kim Fletcher

In 2014, I had the honor to pray with a woman I love and respect deeply. Her name is Sandy Hall and she is a highly prophetic painter who allows her artistic gifting to bring Heaven to earth. After we had spent time praying with two other friends, we sat enjoying the presence of God. While Sandy's eyes were still closed, she reached for each of us and began to speak prophetically. I was last. When she reached me, I took her hand with my left hand simply because it was closest to her right hand. Eyes STILL closed, she quickly released my hand and said, *"Give me your writing hand."* If I had not been tuned in closely to what God was saying and doing, I could have easily thought she said, *"Give me your right hand."* But she clearly asked for the hand with which I write and she began to speak that she saw books coming from my hand.

That account was the first thing to come to my mind as

I sit down for the first time after humbly accepting Lauren's offer to join her in penning her journey and making it available to you.

I believe the book you hold in your hand is, in part, a fulfillment of Sandy's prophetic eye "seeing" messages flowing from my heart that would release transformation to a generation of individuals who are hungry to experience more of God and more from this life.

I have been invited to assist in writing other stories and have turned most offers down. To put your name on a written work is to say that you are in agreement with the content and the intended purpose.

You might wonder why I said YES to this project. That is quite simple. I quickly saw past what might be perceived as just another survivor's story to the heart of what has compelled Lauren (and her mother, Susan) to revisit the deep emotional and physical pain of 2014 in order to make this story accessible to you.

Many people have survived devastating challenges. But few come out on the other side, still bearing scars but determined to allow those scars to be a platform of influence and inspiration. It would be much easier perhaps for Lauren to just go on with her life.

Herein lays the true gift of her story and the highest power of this book. You hold in your hands the gateway to enter into all that Lauren had to attain by agony, pain and an ongoing struggle that she is still living out today … she paid the price for you to hold her insights in your hand and she selflessly now passes the lessons learned onto you for the meager cost of a book. The price she still pays daily is substantial.

You didn't have to live this story. All you have to do is join her journey by reading, and then simply ask one question, *"God, why did you place this story in my hands? How would you have me to live out what is about to be revealed to me?"*

Before you read on, you should be cautioned to some of what you might be walking into. God has worked many deep and abiding heart transformations into this amazing young woman. She is now walking in a higher level of her purpose. Her faith is still going deeper. She experienced the pain of abusive treatment after waking from a coma only to find herself being challenged to forgive as Christ forgave. She has been awakened to the power of every breath and she is now fully aware of the fact that every day, God expects something more of each of us than we might have originally imagined.

This story is not one to be read and quickly forgotten. *It is intended to impact the way you live and the gratitude with which you approach all of life.*

I have joined this journey as a Messenger and Ambassador of Jesus. I believe partnering to tell this story is a Kingdom Assignment that Jesus personally crafted for me as His daughter.

I don't believe that God kept Lauren alive against all odds in order to "use her" for His Kingdom. I believe He breathed life back into her in order to awaken His Kingdom within her by way of His Spirit, releasing His daughter into her full destiny to bring identity, hope and transformation to those who encounter His Story through her eyes.

As a woman of deep faith, Lauren would have been promoted if she had not survived. She would have awakened in the presence of God to a glorified body. At many points over the past year, dying would have been the easy way out, but God left her here for a purpose and has captured her heart with the commission to tell her story. She is now self-lessly inviting you into her story. She is not writing to get famous, but to make the One who brought her back from the brink of death famous and to remind you that when you may feel your life is almost over, the final word has not been spoken. Victory is inevitable for those who hold onto the lifeline she discovered.

His name is Jesus and He destined for you to be holding this book at this time. Let it take you deeper into your highest destiny. Allow it to awaken you to the deep significance of a love relationship with your Father. As sons and daughters of the Most High King, we have been created for far more than most could ever imagine.

Then don't forget to thank Jesus (and Lauren) for allowing the insights to come without having to suffer as she has suffered.

Actually, we are aware that some of you may be in a challenging season of life as you read. Lauren and I have a special heart for those for which this story will be a lifeline to hope.

Miracles come in different forms. Some people are healed and delivered instantly. And some are healed as part of an ongoing process by faith. One of the greatest miracles of all is having true friends to share this journey. Know that we stand with you as friends, praying this over you:

"Father, we believe that each person reading this story is reading it by Your design. We ask for You to meet each individual in a personal and powerful way. Release faith, hope and transformation. Unlock destinies. Give blueprints of purpose to those who have felt "less than." Awaken us to live in a way that honors You for giving us a life that we have been guilty of taking for granted. Show us Your highest plans. Equip us by your Holy Spirit to live in such a selfless way that we choose to lay down the right to our own stories and allow you to use them in any way you desire to build others up into all they were created to be."

When Sandy released my hand, I took time to write down what she had shared. Today, I am reminded that this book was being seen before it existed. I did not know Lauren in 2014. Even then, she was fighting for her life. But God knew! And here we are together to remind you that your story is far from over. Keep reading. Keep living. And remember that the best is always yet to come.

—Kim Fletcher
Award-winning author of *The Tension Point,*
Don't Miss Your Boat and *Your Exceptional Life Begins Now*

TUNNEL OF CHANGE

CHAPTER 1

"Faith never knows where it is being led,
but it loves and knows the One who is leading."
—*Oswald Chambers*

I have always loved the Super Bowl. In 2014 the game was played on February 2nd at Met Life Stadium with the Seattle Seahawks winning over the Denver Broncos. It was their first Super Bowl win. The final score was 43 to 8. (Wikipedia)

As much as I love football, I missed the 2014 game for a good reason. I was in a coma fighting for my life. *Can you believe it? I slept through one of my favorite sporting events of the year.*

I love seeing the players merge onto the field out of the tunnel that connects the lockers and strategy rooms to the field. The energy with which they enter the game is inspiring and uplifting. They are about to have the ultimate chance to prove how effective their training was on the other side of that tunnel … it is game time and they all have on their game faces.

31

The players in the 2014 Super Bowl followed that tradition as they ran onto the field, full of energy and expectation, ready to win a championship and obtain the famed Super Bowl ring. While the Seahawks and Broncos stormed the field wearing their best game faces, I was headed into a tunnel of a different sort. While they ran out into the bright lights of a stadium full of fans, I was headed into darkness deeper than I had ever imagined. Much like the players, I was about to find out how well my life's training had equipped me for the challenges that lie ahead.

Playing is easy when you can see victory in sight. It is another thing altogether to stay focused and determined to come from behind. That is where my game began … far behind, with all odds stacked against me.

Whether or not you like football, we all love to see a player come from behind to win. That unexpected shift carries the power to cause die-hard fans to begin cheering for another team or player. Loss, pain and misfortune have a way of uniting us into a formidable force.

Much like when a team comes from behind to win a game, I know that I am here to share this story largely because a great stadium full of fans in the form of family, friends, medical staff and God Himself came alongside and refused to let me lose in defeat.

One of my inspirations through this journey has been Judy Siegle. Judy became a quadriplegic after a drunk driver ran into her car just after she graduated from high school. As she faced the loss of her dream of playing college basketball, she courageously declared, *"The game may be different.*

But the game must go on." She goes on in her powerful book, *Living Without Limits,* to tell how she had to redirect her attention quickly off of what had been lost and shift her heart onto what lies ahead.

This is my story, told from the same perspective. I have no desire for my story to attract pity or sorrow. I want it to direct your attention forward in your own life. We have all experienced loss and disappointments in varying forms. The real question is, what will you do with what remains? Will you give in to depression, despair and apathy? Or will you choose the path of the champion ... rising out of the ashes to win?

I invite you into my story ... first into the dark tunnel that threatened to rob me of my life, then into the glorious light somewhere on the other side. What began as a tragedy has now become my conviction that my best days are ahead.

Unlike my Super Bowl heroes, I'm not playing for a medal or a ring. I am still fighting for my life.

It is a joy unimaginable to be alive today with the opportunity to move forward into hope. But before I can move on, I feel compelled to do something I had never dreamed of doing before this journey ... I feel compelled to capture my story in the form of the book you now hold in your hands so that you can be inspired to stay in the game.

While in the dark of a coma, unable to speak to express my needs or defend by own dignity, I held onto the hope that game day would come and I would emerge out of the tunnel onto the field into the clearing where a crowd that gathered to cheer me could now share in the story. Well, game day is here. In fact, one full year has cycled and the Super Bowl just aired for the 2015 game. I was awake against all odds and enjoyed watching more than ever.

Few are ever allowed to view what goes on during the training, strategizing and disciplining that shape a few individuals into a team with champion qualities. We just see the final result as players gather on the field to battle it out. Welcome to the dark place where my life's toughest game was about to begin …

SECRETS OF THE TUNNEL

Welcome to the tunnel that encapsulates my last year of life. I will need a bit of assistance in the beginning. During the initial months, a medically-induced coma and a tracheotomy (a tube surgically inserted in my neck to sustain my breathing) silenced my voice.

While I had no voice, my mother became my voice and my scribe. She also took up the daunting dual role as my highest advocate and my lead intercessor. Randy Clark once said, *"If you would consider yourself a follower of Jesus, you are qualified to walk in God's healing power."* I was about to need my Mother's faith and her belief in supernatural healing like never before.

Much like a great coach during the grueling season of training, she took notes daily on all of the major events. She motivated and inspired me, kept track of my fans (logging every gift, every card, every visit, every phone call), and kept the team of professionals on their tip toes. She single handedly directed an orchestra of events while somehow managing to keep her head above water. Most importantly, she kept the entire team – myself included – focused on the only One who could bring us to victory, Jesus Christ. She penned her prayers of faith and frustration almost daily over the weeks and months to come.

Wise athletes always give credit to those who trained them and inspired them. If I just played the hardest game of my life, then my mom would be awarded the title of "head coach." She was living every parent's worst nightmare as she stood and stayed by my hospital bed. The next few pages are my story of those early days of this fight as seen through her eyes. The details you are about to read were painstakingly penned daily by the hand of a mother in agony over the real fact that her only daughter could die any day. Or perhaps I would awaken in the end only to wish I had died.

This is as much her story as it is my own.

A MOTHER'S WORST NIGHTMARE

CHAPTER 2

"Great faith doesn't come out of great effort,
but out of great surrender."
—*Bill Johnson*

I am Susan Parker. These days, I am known to most as "Lauren's Mom." Just over a year ago, we were all living peaceful and joy-filled lives. Every morning just about 7:45, my phone would ring as I was commuting to work. I would pick up the phone, fully expecting to hear my beloved daughter say once again, *"Hey, Mom!"* That is the way my day began for many years. For about fifteen minutes as we both headed into work, we would chat, laugh and start each other's day with the joy only known between a mother and a daughter.

That simple daily tradition we had taken for granted was about to come under attack.

On Sunday, January 12th, 2014, our day began differently with a trip to the emergency room (ER). Nothing is peskier than catching a virus. Lauren was given a breathing treatment and sent home with antibiotics and steroids from a local hospital. Instead of improving, the symptoms got worse. The voice I always expected to be filled with joy and mischief was becoming tinged with fear. When she called on January 14th, 2014, just a couple of days after that initial trip to the ER, I took Lauren back to the doctor. She was given another breathing treatment as the simple process we take for granted became labored and difficult. She was then sent to the hospital for admission.

I almost felt relieved … now she could get the treatment she needed, get over this virus and get on with her life. After all, isn't that what usually happens when you catch a cold, the flu or even pneumonia?

On our way to the hospital, we stopped to grab a sandwich and called her father, Lum, my former husband. Little did we know that he was about to join our fight for her life and become a key player. We headed to the emergency room where it took seven agonizing hours to get her settled into a room, initially diagnosed with pneumonia which had already invaded several areas in her lungs.

RE-OCCURING NIGHTMARE

If there is anything worse than a bad dream, it is one that keeps coming back again and again. The very next day, only a few short days into this journey, Lauren seemed much weaker. Everything she did, simple things, totally drained her energy. I began asking to have her transferred to a larger hospital where she could receive specialized treatment. The reply brought a shock-wave of REALITY. Her doctor simply stated, *"She is not stable enough to be moved."* This was all so confusing.

My heart sank as I heard her first doctor say again, *"Well, she looks good on paper, but…"* What did that even mean? The diagnostic details may have looked promising, but Lauren was looking weaker by the hour. A full day had now passed from the time I asked for her to be moved or have a specialist get involved.

Wow! What a shock. I began to have those internal conversations with myself where your mind wants to wander to the darkest imaginable scenario, only to have your spirit argue that things will be OK. What and who could I believe? What should I be doing differently?

Lauren's life was now on the line. Every decision began to feel like a matter of life or death.

It occurred to me and to her father, just lay people, that there was no pulmonary specialist on her case. The advocate that lay dormant somewhere inside most every mom began to rise up. I ASKED! I was shocked at the response. I was told by hospital personnel that Lauren would have to ask for herself due to the new privacy laws. I reminded them that she is held captive by her body in that room just down the hall, so could they please go ask her. They did not follow up with Lauren but the order was secured anyway. The early bureaucracy was enough to make me nauseated. I am sure glad then that I had no idea how many times over the next few months that I would be required to fight this uphill political nonsense … that very thought would have buried me in hopelessness.

Here came the new doctor to her room. *"Now we would get the help she needed,"* was my hope-filled thought. Yet again, we had to answer the exact same questions … I was

39

beginning to wish we had the initial story on a recorder so we could just push the "play" button. I pondered, why couldn't the high tech medical world find a simple solution to this grueling interrogation process that makes sick and weak individuals feel like criminals being questioned in a court room? It was painful enough to be living it, only to have to re-live it verbally over and over again.

At 3:00 am the next day, Lauren sat slump shouldered in the shower hoping the water would stimulate her breathing. The mom in me felt a deepening sense of concern. This is far more serious than we imagined. *"God, please guide us in the right way to get Lauren the best care."* I prayed at her bedside not knowing how many times that scene was going to repeat itself in the coming months. While there were great staff and doctors, I knew her only hope was in God now showing up and heading the team caring for her at this critical juncture.

The challenges of that day were offset by visitors. I marveled early on at how certain individuals carried uniquely precious gifts. One is still known today as the one who brought laughter … her name is Teresa and this day was no exception. Another friend carried the gift of song. Faithful friends and family would become a lifeline to the outside world as we were being pulled deeper and deeper into this tunnel of darkness, a place Lauren now refers to as her "Tunnel of Change."

My induction into this process taught me one thing early on – you have to be proactive and strong with hospital personnel. A patient without an advocate feels a bit like a boat on an open sea without a rudder or a map to guide its direction. I was already beginning to feel a bit sea sick, as I started being labeled as the "difficult mom." No one really wanted to deal with me.

"Jesus, what is going on here?", I prayed. Pneumonia should only last 3-4 days, then a bit of rest at home while you recover. This is much more serious. Thursday, January, 16th, 2014, my fears were reinforced as she was transferred to the Intensive Care Unit (ICU) to be placed on a ventilator to assist her with breathing. It was room 523. I remember it as if it were yesterday.

Her pulmonary doctor was now joined by an infectious disease doctor. Together, they decided to medically induce a coma and complete paralysis in order to allow her body to rest in hopes of stimulating healing. Lung samples were sent to Atlanta for further analysis, almost as if the doctors were investigators trying to deduce a crime scene. What was happening and why was this happening were the seemingly unanswerable questions of the day.

Her final words included her desire to not be left on a ventilator long-term if something should go wrong. Her father and I were asked to leave her room while the ventilator was inserted. No longer able to speak, Lauren was asked to surrender her cell phone.

My heart was breaking into a million pieces. This can't be happening! She was about to lose her voice, her ability to speak for herself at a time when we needed to hear her thoughts more than ever. While standing in the hall, I looked back and our eyes met. She waved. This girl is my love and my world! God be with her. This nightmare was shaking us to our core.

We were allowed to visit her later that evening. The ventilator tube was down her throat. I have never felt so divided. While this machine could help her breath, it seemed almost barbaric. I actually thought my heart would rip inside my own chest. How did my precious girl get so sick so quickly? What would happen if she now got choked but was unable to tell anyone? The questions seemed to be outweighing answers at this stage.

My journals from those days included a long list of visitors that day. We prayed constantly at Lauren's bedside. We were asked to remove all personal belongings from her room. The walk to the car to take away those items felt like hundreds of miles. As we placed everything in the car, a yellow balloon with a smiley face escaped and took off for the sky. That broke my heart ... would my precious daughter ever smile or know that kind of freedom again? Please Lord, let Lauren LIVE!

Now, she didn't even have the simple comforts of a personalized room to rest in. She was held captive in a highly-mechanized room that looked more like a place of torture.

Friday, January 17th, 2014 was the first full day in ICU. Lauren appeared calm and comfortable; however, I could not stop thinking about what she must be feeling and thinking. Those thoughts were tormenting in this season when she had no way to communicate.

DARK DAYS AHEAD

A feeding tube is now added so she won't starve to death while in this medially-induced sleep. Again, the list of visitors and calls was long. This early wave of support was creating a momentum of love that would carry us far into the dark days ahead.

Despite those who came and went, a deep and somber responsibility took hold of my heart … I am her only voice right now. I pray to know how to facilitate her getting the best care. I do this all out of love.

You learn things you never knew before in situations such as this, like the simple fact that a latex allergy can be life threatening. Lum, her Dad, was making friends with the nurses over discussions about formerly unfamiliar items like the distinctions of fabric tape and paper tape. Tape, gloves, supplies, and even bubble gum all contain latex. Who knew?

Lauren ran a fever today. I worry about her body being overloaded with this barrage of medicine. I never dreamed she could be SO SICK! While steadfast and determined to trust God, I still felt the pain of a broken heart. I would have traded places with her in a moment.

We are now constantly being told, *"This could get worse before it gets better"* along with, *"If she survives, it will be a long recovery process."*

I just want a guarantee she will recover. I have the time to help her. I just need His grace to give us the opportunity. *"Oh God, just assure me she is going to live."* We pray more at her bedside. I know this is her only hope.

Saturday, she had a great male nurse. He helped me wash her hair. He was a true gift as an encourager. No fever today. Another long list of visitors were logged, causing me to realize how many true friends she has and how her life has already impacted many.

Lauren struggles, fighting the tubes. I whisper for her to stay calm, trying to remind her that this is all needed to get her well. *"Oh God, please help her."* She is in real trouble here, but this is not too big for God. I can hardly bear seeing her so sick. I thank God for every ounce of strength He is giving me. I could not ride this roller coaster alone as Lauren does better one day only to lose ground the next.

She is now in a specialized bed that helps to prevent skin from breaking down in individuals who are unable to move voluntarily. It vibrates while moving side to side. I find my-self thanking God for equipment like this that is helping her.

Sunday, just one week after this nightmare began, we are told that churches everywhere have been alerted and are now praying with us. Her army of support was growing. Her doc-tor feels her chances of survival are great. She has no fever this day. Other doctors on the team don't seem as enthusi-astic. It is hard to know who and what to believe. I logged a long list of visitors again this day. Many of us gathered to pray, as Heather began to sing *Amazing Grace.* The comfort that filled the waiting area where we gathered was super-natural, a reminder and declaration that God is in control!

Yet, even in the midst of great comfort, doubt and fear tried to assault my heart. I had to constantly remind myself that fear is not from God, but from our adversary. I declare that God is the One in control over and over again.

People we had never met were praying and sending word of their concern. A powerful thought captures my heart …

This God I am trusting loves Lauren more than I ever could. She is in His hands. I choose to believe that He will honor these prayers.

The doctor asked to meet us in the chapel. He told us again how life threatening this is. He wanted to do scans of her lungs but was unable as she could not be moved in her current condition. Tomorrow would bring the results of tests done on her lungs. Perhaps that would give direction and answers.

Monday arrives only for us to learn that the tests containing samples from lung tissue were botched somewhere along the way. My daughter lay fighting for her life, with every moment counting and critical tests were botched. More than ever now, God is my only hope!

LEARNING TO SPEAK LIFE

Our former pastor and dear friend, Nathan L. May, had watched Lauren grow up. He entrusted me with a list of wonderful scripture passages to read over her. I encouraged her daily with the Word of God and assured her that she is doing everything right and that the rest is up to God. I have to believe she hears me … I have to believe He hears me too!

More visitors, more snacks and more gifts. But Lauren cannot enjoy any of them. Again, I am reminded that so many are coming to share love with Lauren because she had first been a friend to them.

"For God loved the world in this way: He gave His One and Only Son, so that everyone who believes in Him will not perish but have eternal life." John 3:16

There you lay with no voice. You were not even awake, and yet it was clearly evident that you were being loved now by so many because the Jesus in you had reached out to them when you were able. You had lived by the verse that teaches us to *"Do unto others as you would have them do to you."*

Each visit, each day, I tell you:

I love you in big ways

I love you in small ways

I love you this minute

I'll love you always

You are my precious daughter. I love you. I pray at your bedside. Giving up is not an option. I choose to believe you WILL BE HEALED. I turn to a few favorite passages to strengthen my own resolve.

"The Lord is my light and my salvation – whom should I fear? The Lord is the stronghold of my life – of whom should I be afraid?" Psalm 27:1

"God is our refuge and strength, a helper who is always found in times of trouble. Therefore we will not be afraid." Psalm 46: 1,2b

"Do not fear, for I am with you; do not be afraid, for I am your God. I will strengthen you; I will help you; I will hold on to you with My righteous right hand." Isaiah 41:10

Today is January 21st, just eleven days since this ordeal began. It feels like eleven years. We are told again by one of the doctors that her chances of surviving are good. Her pneumonia has cleared but she now has Adult Respiratory

Distress Syndrome, the most severe form of Acute Respiratory Distress Syndrome (ARDS). The ARDS, they said, was caused by the H1N1 flu. The bad news we received is that ARDS is associated with a long recovery time. What a nightmare. What can go wrong seems to be going wrong. How can this be happening to my sweet, precious Lauren?

Again, friends gathered to pray as Heather sang about the Blood of Jesus. Thank you God for bringing your strength at just the right times to keep us positioned in faith and not fear. Oh how I wish Lauren could eat the M & M's one friend brought to her today. It makes me smile, knowing how much she likes one of the M & M characters.

We place a CD player in her room and begin playing some of her favorite music to comfort and reassure her. I pray asking God to hold her in the palm of His hand, ministering to her moment by moment with His presence. I asked Him to allow Lauren to feel His love like never before.

I have honestly never seen anything like this outpouring from churches, friends, family, co-workers and pastors. Our family is definitely growing!

It is now Wednesday as Lauren seemed to improve slightly. Taken off of one medication, I feel a glimmer of hope and decide to head out to Lauren's house since it was close-by where Lum could cut my hair… Lauren would think this is so funny! She is the hair dresser and has kept me in stylish cuts. I figure that her dad would be the next most qualified, as he has been a barber for many years.

Thursday, January 23rd brings bad news of fluid collecting in her fragile lungs. All this while yet another important lung test had been botched. How can this keep happening? While another sample is taken and sent to be studied, the doctor assures us she is receiving medicine to cover any germ/infection that this may be. That is part of what concerns me at this stage, the tremendous amounts of medicine being infused into her body. Again, the visitor list is long with people coming from her office, multiple churches, family, even her personal hair stylist.

I continue to ask God to bring her out of this and to keep her from having fear while she is in the dark place of a coma. I can't help but wonder what she knows, what she hears, what she feels. Will I ever know?

Her fever is up and this marks Friday, January 24th. Now her stomach was swelling due to the abundance of fluid accumulating and a possible complication of a bowel obstruction. Again, we are told that she needs further testing that she is not stable enough to endure. She is too fragile for a CAT scan or for even being transported to another part of the hospital. The doctor warned us that the swelling is likely to worsen. Her daisies and balloons are in the waiting area, cheering up everyone but Lauren, the one who needs them most.

"Please God, she looks so pitiful now. She doesn't deserve this." The honest and raw pleas of a mother's heart were all I had to offer. I begged God to sustain her life and return her to us. My niece reminds me of a precious truth I would cling to many times in the days ahead: *"When God's all we've got, He's all we need."* What a wonderful assurance. We pray more at her bedside.

Saturday, January 25th was full of sorrow. The swelling

got much worse and Lauren developed complications with her left eye and the right side of her chest due to a reaction to a new treatment. She continued to fight with the tubes in her mouth despite the medically-induced paralysis, while I constantly remind her that these are needed to get her well. I know she is strong and she is fighting.

The doctor assures us that the complications are not bowel related. While that is good news, it does not solve the mystery of why these complications keep occurring.

We are barraged with gifts, flowers and food. While I will be forever grateful for the love and support that sustained us, all I wanted was for her to recover. It was hard to find the emotional strength to share joy and gratitude with those who came while not knowing from day to day if she would even survive. Sunday, January 26th is marked by worsening swelling and another long list of visitors. We washed her hair, sang and prayed. Heather's songs today speak of Peace, Wonderful Peace.

We are told that the swelling will not reduce until the lungs begin to heal. *"God, that is your job. Please heal her lungs in a mighty way."* I take time to reveal to the doctors and staff that we have prayed for them to have wisdom and for Him to direct their decisions and their care of Lauren. I had to hold onto the belief that when it felt we were losing ground, God was surely a step ahead of the rest. He was never late in showing up. He was always on time. I held to this promise.

One morning I arrived to visit Lauren but was not allowed to due to an emergency in ICU. My immediate thought was, *"Is it Lauren?"* I walked around the corner praying and one of the housekeepers came through the door. It is important to note that this particular person had committed to pray for Lauren. She went on to assure me that she had just seen Lauren and that she looked good and was resting. I knew Jesus was present and that He placed this woman there for me – just on time!

A doctor is coming on for a week and we are warned, *"He is a jerk."* *"Oh God, we don't need this right now. Please have mercy on us."*

The "jerk" turns out to be dealing with painful personal issues. He is an excellent doctor and encourages us by trying some new strategies as we choose to pray for peace to come into his life. This was one of the times when I caught a glimpse of how this tragic situation was placing us in the path of others who needed to be encouraged as well.

At this stage, a good day is simply one when I realize in the morning that I did not receive the dreaded middle-of-the-night call. She is still alive. I thank our Loving God that she still has a chance to emerge out of this dark tunnel.

On Tuesday, January 28th, the swelling was down some. While that was good news, her oxygen levels were also down. That was bad news as it meant she did not have enough oxygen getting to her blood. A diagnosis of H1N1 influenza was also confirmed. I found myself going head to head with the doctor referred to as the "hospitalist" who did not want to call the pulmonary doctor that I wished to be included. She finally did call and he made critical adjustments in the setting of the ventilator.

I had to sleep in the chapel due to snow. The snow couldn't stop the visitors. The list was twenty-four strong just this one day.

Twenty-one people come again on Wednesday, January 29th. I continually talk to Lauren, trusting she is hearing me. I find myself hoping she can smell my perfume so she knows I am here with her. The roller coaster continues, as she improves one minute only to crash the next. She is sedated today to allow her body to rest more deeply.

The next day, the swelling is almost gone. Her dad keeps poking her body as he performs his own "medical analysis" of the situation. Men! I told him I wish she would wake up and pop him, declaring for him to stop. While his unique way of being present tended to drive me a bit crazy, he was fully present and for that I was most grateful. I knew that Lauren would be so blessed if she were aware of how he had been right here with us.

GOD RECRUITS HIS TEAM

Friday, January 31st marked a possible milestone. The doctor declared that she might be turning a corner and a new doctor was being added to the team, Dr. Neveen M. Habashi. I tell Lauren how much I want to see her blue eyes and her million-dollar smile. *"Lord, please let it be soon!"*

This new doctor is sent to "fill in" while other doctors are away at a seminar. I know in my heart that she needs to be at a specialty facility and I cannot stand the idea of someone simply filling in. I expect the worst, only to realize that God had just delivered a key member of the team from a tiny hospital that I had failed to respect.

We pass the days with more visits, and an abundance of food and love.

Sunday, February 2nd was the last day with the doctor we expected to be a jerk. He had turned out to be a huge blessing. Lauren rested well that day. I am growing desperate to hear her sweet voice. Plans begin to be discussed about eventually transferring Lauren to a facility that specializes in treating patients on ventilators.

Dr. Habashi arrived, assessed the situation and gave us three options:

1. Continue treatment unchanged

2. Move her to another hospital

3. Pursue a different method of treatment at this facility

She went on to say that it was going to be critical to begin reducing the medicines that have kept Lauren unable to respond in order to begin seeing what she is left with at this stage. She went on to share that she felt Lauren had a 50/50 chance of survival and her overall prognosis was not good according to science; however, this precious doctor always encouraged us to believe for the best outcome.

As we prayed for wisdom in the chapel, we felt God lead us to choose the third option. We would quickly realize that this doctor was not a small-town "fill in" but rather a God send! Of all the people who were qualified to fill in, the Lord delivered us a physician whose brother, also a physician, just happened to be involved in ARDS research at the University of Maryland. He was now being consulted. We called this our double blessing! A deep sense of relief flooded Lauren's room as Dr. Habashi patiently stayed with her over two hours obtaining the baseline information she would need to guide her care forward.

More visitors come and go as the doctors now begin to discuss a surgical procedure that would place a tracheotomy in her neck in order to get the ventilator tube out of her mouth. One doctor felt it would be easier to wean her off of this form of breathing assistance eventually. While there were possible benefits, there were also the risks of infection and scar tissue.

Lauren opens her eyes some now but does not make eye contact. We encourage her to stay calm and we reassure her she is improving.

The next day, Dr. Habashi tells us her lungs are improving. I am so thankful for this woman. She is in Lauren's room often, never rushes away, makes machine adjustments herself and shows so much concern. She has been sent by God, reminding me that He is here every step of the way.

Lauren's co-workers began planning a benefit for Lauren in March at a coffee house and also a yard sale/cook out/bake sale to donate funds to her medical expenses. As wonderful as these friends were, such offers and plans caused me to realize that we were in for an extended journey. Would we have the stamina and faith needed to run to the finish line? Again, faith and the Word of God were my only anchors. I was reminded how Jesus and many of his disciples ran a good race and finished well...

"Don't you know that the runners in a stadium all race, but only one received the prize? Run in such a way to win the prize." I Corinthians 9:24

"Therefore, since we also have such a large cloud of witnesses surrounding us, let us lay aside every weight and the sin that so easily ensnares us. Let us run with endurance the race that lies before us, keeping our eyes on Jesus, the source and perfector of our faith, who for the joy that lay before Him endured a cross and despised the shame and has sat down at the right hand of God's throne." Hebrews 12:1

DIVORCE COULDN'T DIVIDE

"God is arming the Body of Christ with weapons of His divine love that the enemy has no defense against."
—*Bob Jones*

Dr. Habashi called me and Lauren's father great coaches. Considering that we were not always great at being a team in the past, this was a hard-won compliment and one that I took a great deal of comfort in at this stage in Lauren's journey.

Despite a divorce years before, we had become friends and now she needed us to be "together" as we stayed at the hospital almost around the clock. We talked together, prayed together and encouraged her. She deserved our love, not our division at this desperate time.

We were fortunate, despite being divorced when Lauren was a young girl, that we always understood the importance of becoming friends for the sake of our daughter having access to both of us. Our roots of faith kept us anchored to a mutual commitment to parent her from a place of love and forgiveness. We had given Lauren the gift of parents who, now years later, would be able to show up and visit together, pray together in unity, while placing her needs ahead of our own. The commitments to friendship that we made in her childhood continued to serve us well, as the two of us, along with my friend Wayne and Lauren's step-mother, Donata, saw that Lauren was never left alone in the early weeks.

If I could encourage couples going through this nightmare who have perhaps separated or divorced, I would encourage them to forgive, let go and get pride out of the way so that the person in need can be blessed as we knew Lauren deserved. She needed both of her parents. We couldn't live together outside of this situation, but now that we were thrown into it, we owed it to her to put our own issues aside so she could have her family together cheering her on as a powerfully united force.

My friend, Wayne, drove Lauren's dad and me back and forth to the various hospitals daily. But, being together every day, we could easily get on each other's nerves. One day, I joked with a nurse who was a single mom, saying, *"Every morning when I wake up, the first thing I do is thank God my daughter is alive. The second thing I do is thank God that I don't have to go home with either of these men."* The tension of this season welcomed any comic relief. We both laughed!

On Wednesday, February 5th, the swelling began to return and one doctor announced he felt it was too dangerous to remove the ventilator and surgically insert the tracheotomy. Things were not working in her favor. She seemed anxious. I can tell as she restlessly and pointlessly moves her arms and legs and has a "frightened" look in her eyes. I coach her to breathe deep and slow. Her dad gets confused and tells her to breathe short and deep … we laugh. Any relief to the weight of this awful situation feels like a tiny gift.

Thirty people came to visit that day. As grateful as I was, at times, it felt a bit like being awakened out of a deep sleep and thrown on stage to conduct an entire orchestra. Only one problem. I don't know how to conduct an orchestra. Perhaps God was teaching and equipping me supernaturally.

Thursday, February 6th was one of those days that felt like the valley on the roller coaster. The ventilator tube was not in correctly, the ventilator had to be re-adjusted, a chest tube had to be inserted to remove air and fluid, placing her at further risk of infection and more pneumonia. Her blood work reveals that her kidneys may be sustaining damage from the assault of bed rest and massive amounts of medication. Her oxygen levels keep dropping and I find myself having to prod the staff to pay closer attention to the monitors.

The following day brings another fever and it is Dr. Habashi's last day. Lauren's eyes seem to cry out, *"Help me mom." "God, I wish I could but I am so thankful that YOU can since I cannot."* Dr. Habashi promised to take us to dinner when Lauren is well. She was such a wonderful and compassionate gift on this rugged journey. I assure her that we will come visit her when Lauren is able. This simple future plan gave me reason to hope in Lauren's full recovery. Those simple links to the future, a bright future, often kept me able to put one foot in front of the other.

Finally, a few new procedures and strategies seem to be paying off. I can hardly bear this new season of her gaining some awareness only to be awake enough to panic as she realizes where she is over and over again as she comes and goes from sleep. I know she is afraid. All I know to do is pray.

Saturday, February 8th, an x-ray shows some improvement in her lungs. She had to have a blood transfusion. Trying to lighten the day with humor, her friend Teresa said she was going to tell Lauren that it came from her. The doctor explains three stages of ARDS and that Lauren is between stages two and three. We ask him to call Dr. Habashi as the swelling again returns.

I grow more and more concerned over the effect that the massive doses of steroids, antibiotics and pain medication are having on her body overall. Lying in the bed so long has to also take a grave toll on the body. *"Lord, please don't let her organs or her mind be damaged by this assault."* We prayed endlessly at her bedside.

Lauren continued to open and close her eyes, but she never seemed to focus. They sedate her more so she can rest, but it troubles me to see her so still, so lifeless. Our dear friend, Heather, arrives again and sings more. It is as if God supplied us with His own worship team through her. I wonder if she realizes the mighty way God is using her to lift us out of this pit into His glorious hope? Psalm 103: 1-5 echoes the blessings to come that her heart of worship kept us believing for…

"My soul, praise Yahweh, and all that is within me, praise His holy name. My soul, praise the Lord, and do not forget all His benefits. He forgives all your sin; He heals all your diseases. He redeems your life from the pit; He crowns you with faithful

love and compassion. He satisfies you with goodness; your youth is renewed like the eagle."

One thing was for sure. Lauren was preparing to receive quite a glorious crown and I was sure going to need my youth to be renewed. It had now been less than a month, but the month felt more like a year.

More haircuts from barber Lum, more candy, more visitors and more bad news. The doctor feels the tracheotomy is inevitable and that the vent tube must be removed. The x-rays are worse again. One of the doctors told me to let them do their job. Before I can censor myself, I ask the only question that comes to mind. *"Do you have children?"* That is my only reply to my proactive and assertive behavior. My word to all caregivers and patient advocates is to never back down when your intuition tells you to press in. I am not advocating disrespect … I am simply advocating each person's need for a loving advocate who cannot be bullied or overpowered.

I am not taking credit where credit is not due, but I am confident that certain procedures and team members were secured for Lauren because this mother was someone's worst nightmare. I kept reminding them that we are living our worst nightmare while they were doing a job by choice.

I comforted myself to know that at least she will be relieved of this dreadful tube down her throat. Tears run from the side of her eyes, as my heart continues to break.

On Tuesday, February 11th, I sign the consent for the tracheotomy procedure to be done on the 12th. *"Lord, please heal her lungs and give her the strength to wake up."*

The nurses try to assure me that this is my nightmare,

not Lauren's. That she is unaware. My heart knows otherwise when I look into her eyes. I begin to wonder what she thinks and if she dreams. I tell her that angels are singing over her and to her. I need her to wake up so we can know what is going on inside of her.

The procedure is done the next morning at 7:30 am. While the doctors feel confident this was the right way to go, her increase in blood pressure and heart rate make me wonder. The doctor begins to discuss moving her to another facility eventually where she can hopefully be weaned off of the ventilator.

Lauren's Dad, Wayne and I all slept in the chapel again due to more snow. In an odd sort of a way, it is a comforting place to sleep. Lauren, you have now slept through two snows and the Super Bowl. The original plan was three or four days in the hospital to treat your pneumonia. That was over a month ago now. How could my precious baby girl sleep and miss a solid month of life? What all will she have to miss before this nightmare is finally over? Will it ever be over?

I whisper encouragement in your ear. I plant the vision of a beach trip. I tell you how strong you are and that you are getting better each day. I tell you over and over:

I love you in big ways

I love you in small ways

I love you this minute

I'll love you always

Lauren ran a fever and we sleep again at the hospital's

hospitality house. We are told that hard days lie ahead as she faces physical therapy and the grueling process of learning to breathe on her own again. We are told about a facility in Winston Salem, North Carolina that has special machines which help strengthen the lungs.

Her hemoglobin is low and she required more blood today. A case manager got involved to help map out the plan to transfer her from Hickory to Winston Salem. We are told that she is still not out of danger until she is taken off the ventilator so they could assess the true condition of her lungs.

THIS CRISIS IS REAL

Her oxygen levels drop, her blood pressure and heart rate soar as her fingernails turn blue. We are still in a very real crisis here. Yet, even in the midst of this, God continues to reassure my heart.

Friday, February 14th is Valentine's Day. Lauren opened her eyes more today than any day before. I believe she hears my voice but she does not respond to any directions or commands. Oh, how this concerns my heart. I asked the nurses to not tell her what day it is, as Valentine's is not her favorite holiday.

I cling to promises such as Jeremiah 29:11 ... *"For I know the plans I have for you – this is the Lord's declaration – plans for your welfare, not for disaster, to give you a future and a hope."*

I had to believe that this was not the end and that there was hope ahead for Lauren on the other side of this nightmare. I know one thing for sure about Lauren. If God chooses to keep her here, she will give Him the credit for the miracles we have seen and the ones yet to come. I declared then if God chose to let her live, I was having a "Praise the Lord" party to honor and praise Him. I began to catch a vision for her sharing this story and changing many lives. That hope fueled me to make it yet another day. Some days, I felt energized and hopeful. Other days, I would stand outside the hospital at the front entrance with the four or five steps upward into the main lobby feeling like a climb up Mount Everest.

A fever returns while her hemoglobin returns to normal. Up and down. I feel sea sick again by all the motion.

We find ourselves bonding with other families in crisis as we share countless hours in the waiting area. Lists of visitors and gifts continue to mount.

Saturday, February 15th, I am awakened early by a phone call from the hospital. The nurse tells me that Lauren is collecting fluid again in her lungs. Why is this happening again? More medicine is added to pull off the fluid. How much more can her heart, liver and kidneys endure? Now a rash started with more medicine to counteract that. What medicine do they give when you get allergic to all the medicines? Where does this end?

A nurse contacts the heart surgeon to request that the chest tube be removed. Perhaps it is causing irritation. We are then told that the doctor tried to take her off the sedation medication too quickly and that her symptoms are the result of withdrawal from the prescription drugs. You guessed it.

Another drug is now added to offset the symptoms of detoxification. This all seems enough to cause an addiction to me. How will she ever get free of all this medication?

A representative is being sent to evaluate Lauren as a candidate for the new facility. I stayed with Lauren as she comes off the sedation medication. I told her she was getting better and I asked if she understood. She shook her head *"Yes."* I thanked the Lord for this milestone, our first real communication since January 16th.

Another ray of hope came as I met with Kim, the case worker who told us she was approved by insurance to be transferred to Select Specialty Hospital in Winston Salem where she could hopefully come off the ventilator in time.

I find myself alone in the waiting area reflecting on a day that began with a frightening call that was now ending with hope. This roller coaster seems far from over, but at least today is ending well. An emergency with another patient had required us to leave ICU around 4:30pm. I wait patiently to visit her again at 8:00pm. I love praying at her bedside. It's just my girl, me and God. I am reminded how precious life is. I thank God again for entrusting me with such a precious daughter. What an honor to be her mother. She is one of a kind!

The hospital all seems to be getting involved, asking how she is doing. I began to realize that Lauren was touching lives even while sleeping. How much of an impact would she have when she awakens with a great story to tell? I grow excited thinking of how God might use this ordeal to bring hope to others.

This journey which began on January 12th with a trip to the Emergency Room has now stretched all the way to February 16th, and there is no end in sight. I am always comforted when our favorite nurses are on staff. I feel more at peace when I know she is in good hands. Today, Sunday, was one of those days. John always puts my heart at ease. He is a great encourager and today he uses that gift to push me out the door to Hilton Park.

Map in hand, I'm off with my sandwich, chips and apple to encounter ducks, sunshine and the stark absence of all the sounds and smells that make a hospital so overwhelming. I returned to Lauren resting well. It is concerning me that, while she opens her eyes more, she does not seem to respond much. She did squeeze my hand on command and shook her head *"Yes"* when I asked if she was ready to go to the beach. These tiny victories feel like major battles won, and yet the lack of real communication causes me great concern.

Later that day, she seemed to be trying to talk. John hoped I could interpret. Why is it that everyone thinks that moms have super powers? I grow weary of not being able to understand her.

The Nightmare Shift

CHAPTER 4

"The Lord is my Shepherd, there is nothing I lack ...
even when I go through the darkest valley, I fear no danger,
for you are with me." —Psalm 23: 1,4a

What began as a parent's worst nightmare was about to become Lauren's worst nightmare. The joy of having her begin to awaken slowly is quickly sobered by the harsh realization that she is about to become aware of the magnitude of the challenge she is facing and the devastation that has ravaged her body over the past month.

As the day progresses, Lauren responds a bit more to yes and no questions by nodding her head. Today's bedside prayers focus on asking God for her communication abilities to be strengthened so we can begin to know what she needs and how we can comfort her. My heart grows more concerned with each day passing that she lingers in this dark abyss.

BLACK BOX RECOVERY

Dr. Habashi had been deeply concerned about the

amount of time Lauren would be kept on drugs which altered her alertness. At one point, she indicated that eventually Lauren would have to be awakened in order to see what remained. Another doctor made reference to the black box found at the crash site of an airplane that holds key information on the final few moments leading up to a crash or an emergency landing. We would have no idea what condition her mind or her body was in until she emerged from the grip of this induced coma. Her mind was a bit like that black box, holding the dark secrets of what she was hearing, sensing, experiencing while cut off from all communication with those who stood vigil over her. Would she remember? Would she know us? Would she be able to talk, to move, to recover? I began to long for the day when the sedation would wear off and she would emerge and reveal the secrets held in her little black box. There was only one sobering thought. Would we be able to emotionally handle what that black box would reveal to us? My heart continued to break at the fear of the unknown.

Monday morning, she was trying to talk even more. The doctor is optimistic about the transfer to Select. I try to explain to her that she cannot talk because of the tube in her throat but that will come out soon and then we can communicate better. I asked if she wanted to hear something funny and she shook her head *"yes."* I told her that her dad had cut my hair at her house. She raised her eyebrows and smiled, as if to say, *"Are you kidding me?"* That simple communication brought as much joy as any lengthy conversation we had ever had.

Plans are made for the transfer to occur tomorrow. This

day feels like it marks a milestone for Lauren as she heads out of the traditional hospital and into one equipped to teach her to breathe on her own again. It is a Monday, and yet eighteen visitors come by. One visitor even brought flowers to me. What a wonderful way to end the day!

THE STUBBORN MOTHER

I take time to tell the last shift of nurses goodbye since we will be gone before they return tomorrow. One remarks that the patients who get better often have "Stubborn Mothers." While I was not fond of the label, I had to admit that this label fit. After all, I reminded them that I am her voice and I cannot fail her now!

I also say goodbye to families we have gotten to know who are left behind to continue their hospital vigil. I prepare Lauren to understand that she is moving tomorrow to a place that specializes in getting the tube out so she can talk. She seems to understand. It feels that we have turned a corner. Do I dare to believe?

I find myself whispering this simple prayer:

Oh, dear God, I'm so grateful for all you have done to bring Lauren this far. Your hand has been on her since day one. I see you at work every day. So many people have been touched by her story already. Thank you for every professional who has been involved in her care – and thank you for guiding them with your hand. What a miracle to watch – watching you work! Great things are ahead for Lauren and I give you all of the praise and glory. We could never praise you enough. Thank you, God.

It's been such a wonderful day beginning to really communicate with my precious daughter again. I am so grateful and aware of where this blessing comes from. Lord, put us in places where Lauren's story can be told. We want to tell what wonderful things you have done. You are so good!

I awake. It is Tuesday, February 18th and it is TRANSFER DAY! Lauren is headed to room 6325 at Select Specialty Hospital in Winston-Salem, North Carolina. The doctor we are leaving behind says he is confident she will make daily progress. The staff expresses how much they are going to miss her. Funny, but they didn't say they were going to miss me.

I held the phone to your ear so your dad could talk to you. He was here with you every day until he got sick and I had to be the germ police to keep him away. Oh, how I know you wish you could eat the M&Ms brought to you by a visitor today. Nineteen others also came. The love is overwhelming.

Three o'clock arrives. You respond to the transfer by breaking out in hives. It breaks this mother's heart to know that your skin is now the only way left for your anxiety to make itself known. I asked for you to be given something to calm your nerves and you drift off to sleep. I watch one of your favorite nurses walk out right beside you, guarding you to the very last moment.

The new doctor and nurses come into her new room right away to do a full battery of tests. The doctor is immediately concerned that her left pupil of her eye is not responding. He states he is concerned that she was taken off too much medication too quickly. He reinforces what the first hospital told us about ARDS having a slow recovery time. I remind them that she is allergic to LATEX. They put a sign up over her bed.

The doctor explains to us that the first facility was an acute care hospital while this one is a long term facility, with an average stay of thirty days.

What started out feeling exciting now begins to feel like the second major battle of a much larger war.

Lauren loves the war medals left to her by her grandfather. I wonder what her collection of war medals would look like? She deserves medals for bravery, inspiration, endurance and faith.

When I get ready to leave, now looking at substantial commute distances from home, I ask Lauren what color my coat is. She whispers, *"green."* She was right. She is in there. I have to believe she will be OK. *"God, please help her withdraw safely from all those awful drugs. Please have mercy on her."* It was especially hard to leave her today.

I awake the next day excited to see how she is adjusting to the new surroundings. I arrive in Winston-Salem asking and believing for God to make this her best day yet. I find her needing the nurse's assistance. They take too long to arrive. I begin asking God to help me not be too hard on the staff, while getting Lauren what she needs. Why do you have to work so hard to advocate for a loved one in this situation? Shouldn't there be a minimum standard of care that doesn't place a person at greater risk? *"Lord, give me patience NOW. Lauren is my priority and I feel like a mother lion. I am reminded you are the Lion of Judah. I need you to advocate for her, Lord. Help me to not be labeled here as the stubborn and difficult mom. I just want THE BEST for her. She has been through enough and deserves at least that."*

The staff makes plans to do a CT scan, as the doctor is still concerned that her left eye and left side are not responding correctly. Lauren asks me to help her get up. I explain she is too weak because she has been so sick. She mouthed, *"You can't imagine."* Oh dear Lord, what does she remember? What has this been like for her?

The CT scan is cancelled because her oxygen levels dropped too much when they tried to place her on a portable ventilator to take her to the lab. Several people go into her room to explain what is going on. She grows anxious again. I asked why they had to upset her. They told me it is the law that she be told. I had given her a simple explanation that she was having an x-ray. They explained everything in detail. It was too much for her to take in. The rash returned. The anxiety found a way to "scream out" from her skin. This is breaking my heart.

I thank God for His unconditional love for us as I prepare to leave. I whisper to Lauren:

I love you in big ways

I love you in small ways

I love you this minute

I'll love you always

I arrived the next morning to find Lauren wearing the same gown as the day before and her monitor numbers too high. Mother Lion kicked in. Soon thereafter, she is given meds to bring her vitals down and she is cleaned up. I place a wet cloth on her head to calm her.

I find myself talking to the charge nurse from yesterday about the drama brought on by the "law" stating they had to inform her of every little detail of her care, the incident that led to an anxiety attack. They agree to allow me to be the first to tell Lauren when anything major is about to be done or to be changed. The doctor comes in and notices she is taking too many breaths per minute. She needs the scan done that was cancelled yesterday. An x-ray reveals that her lungs have much healing that needs to happen. The doctor shows me the pictures and explains why he feels she needs to be put back to sleep to allow her body to get extreme, healing rest. What a shock! This can't be happening again. We just started to get her back. We were just beginning to see a little light at the end of this long, dark tunnel. The high hopes that brought us here were quickly reversing back to square one.

I don't know if I can take the heart-break of losing communication with her again after these precious few days of beginning to feel that sweet connection. I place my hope once again in the Only One who has the power to bring us out on the other side of this ongoing, mounting nightmare, God Himself. *"Please Lord, please heal her. I will give You all the praise!"*

The scan is rescheduled for 3:30pm. She is sedated and given extra oxygen. I pray that this event will not overwhelm her body. She is taken and uneventfully, she is returned to her room where orders are given for lights out as she needs rest.

I pray, asking God to prepare us for the results that will be given tomorrow. I ask specifically for there to be no damage to her brain or to her left side. I remind God that I know she is in the palm of His hand. I beg for mercy.

Friday, February 21st, I begin my day by reading Psalm 50 before going to Select. Verse 15 says, *"Call on Me in a day of trouble; I will rescue you, and you will honor Me."* Today would test my ability to hold onto faith, placing more trust in what is unseen than that which is seen.

Before I even arrived, I received a call that she was worse. Her breathing and vitals were not good. She was being moved yet again to the Intensive Care Unit (ICU). Once there, I was given the news that she had a stroke in her posterior cerebral artery which has affected her left side. The scan further confirmed this had occurred while she was hospitalized in Hickory. The doctor reminds me that the ARDS is still more serious even than a stroke. I had to immediately give the situation back to God, choosing to believe healing is coming.

Lauren is so loved that even the distance from home could not limit the visitors. Twenty-one precious friends came this day to encourage, pray and bless us.

The ICU staff is calling her "unstable." The new diagnosis is sepsis, infection which has dangerously traveled into her blood stream, allowing it to circulate throughout her entire body. I'm asked to sign a consent form for an arterial line and a central line to be surgically inserted to help better monitor her entire system. This is overwhelming. I feel sick. All I know to do is pray … I now know God is our only hope. I plead with Him by her bedside:

Today has been so hard, Lord. I feel so sorry for Lauren. God, only you can heal her lungs and that has to happen before she can get well. You are ABLE and you are our ONLY source of healing and hope. You are all we have. Please heal her. She is your child and your love for her is everlasting. Please spare her.

The only way it is even possible for me to leave her side at this point is knowing that when I am not here, Jesus remains by her side.

Through the weekend, I keep whispering for her to rest and fight to get well. How do you rest and fight at the same time? This all feels like too much for her. I remind her that we have much to do together and individually. More tests are done today with more results coming tomorrow. The rash returns and she becomes clammy and wet. I know her body is struggling.

I asked a nurse to please check to see what medicines had been changed that could be linked to the rash returning, but she refused. Mama Lion is about to go on the prowl again. Labels or not, here I come. I feel so alone in this battle to ensure that she is getting the best care possible. I am not a doctor or a nurse, yet it seems like common sense to trace back to the other hospital stay to see what she was taking when she had this reaction before.

While some staff members exercise compassion, those who don't make this fight feel almost unbearable. I barely have the energy to keep showing up. Little do they know that I go into my office at midnight many nights after a full day with Lauren to catch up on the necessities of my day job.

Now they are forcing me to burn emotional reserves I didn't even know I had by being the one who always has to PUSH, PUSH, PUSH!

Now, I begin to hear God speaking back to me. Oh, how I need His friendship to be real:

Susan, "Trust and thankfulness will get you safely through this day. Trust protects you from worrying and obsessing. Thankfulness keeps you from criticizing and complaining, those 'sister sins' that so easily entangle you.

Keeping your eyes on Me is the same thing as trusting Me. It is a free choice that you must make thousands of times daily. The more you choose to trust Me, the easier it all becomes. Thought patterns of trust become etched into your mind. Relegate troubles to the periphery of your mind so that I can remain CENTRAL to your thoughts. Thus, focusing on Me, entrusting your every concern into My care." Sarah Young – Jesus Calling

He went on to encourage me with His Word, taking me to three specific passages.

"Therefore, as you have received Christ Jesus the Lord, walk in Him, rooted and built up in Him and established n the faith, just as you were taught, overflowing with gratitude." Colossians 2:6-7

"But my eyes look to you, Lord God. I seek refuge in You; do not let me die." Psalm 141:8

"...casting all your cares on Him, because He cares about you." I Peter 5:7

God used Donata to direct me to these precious promises. Oh, how I needed this lifeline. "Forgive my doubt, Lord.

My trust is renewed. I choose to trust you completely."

The next day, Lauren's doctor wanted to talk with us. He told us that the longer this goes on, the poorer her prognosis for recovery becomes. I immediately reject this report in my spirit and hold fast to the report of the Lord. I will not be moved. My daughter will be the healed of the Lord. She will recover. God spoke it and I believed it. I had resolved to trust completely.

Today, the natural eye could see erratic vitals and a struggle. My spirit eyes could still see victory coming.

I ask for Dr. Habashi's brother to get involved, but the ego of the man in charge resisted this plan. Seventeen visitors feel like a mighty army standing with us.

The nurse and I bump heads again tonight, literally this time. She dropped a pillow and we both reach to retrieve it. We collide in mid-air. She is a caring woman of faith in God. For this, I am so grateful. It felt so reassuring to leave when she was on duty.

Now I bump heads with Lauren's dad. He thinks I should not be telling her to fight with everything she's got to get better. He was afraid this would cause her to realize how sick she is and that she might give up. I laugh at how protective these parents are being over an adult. We both love her so much. It is hard to know when to push and when to pull back. I need a manual, as no part of life seems to have prepared us for this.

"Lord, you are the Great Physician. You are the One I trust. Bring her through."

THE STRUGGLE TO KEEP HOPE ALIVE

While I am grateful that the doctors are honest and give us information, I also wonder if they are not familiar with how important it is to keep hope alive. I choose more than ever to pay attention to Jesus and Him alone.

Monday brings good news. The blood infection seems to be gone. The sedation is reduced and you start trying to open your eyes. You are so loved! My heart begins to find hope that you will turn a corner this time and move toward healing. I love talking to you and encouraging you. I keep reminding you that we will go to the beach as soon as you are well.

Your nurse today is a mother of six. It is funny how much better I feel when you are cared for by mothers. Your blood pressure goes up when your dad and I talk to you today. I can't begin to imagine why that would affect your blood pressure. After all, I am quite certain he and I have never raised each other's blood pressure. I know you are laughing at us silently. You're probably dreaming of the day when we won't stand over you every moment when this ordeal is finally over.

We leave the room for a few minutes and your vitals stabilize without medication. Maybe that is all you need, for us to leave the room from time to time. Again, I can hear you laughing at us in my heart.

Your sweet nurse tells me a story of a young woman they were preparing to die. Instead, she woke up and fully recovered. She closed her story with the declaration that God is in the miracle business. I ask God to lift us out of the dark into His glorious light.

The miracle is reinforced as the same nurse takes time to show me lung x-rays from a few days ago where Lauren's lungs appeared almost white, an indication of inflammation where oxygen cannot be absorbed. The new pictures show emerging dark coloration, indicating the inflammation is beginning to clear somewhat. What a joy to have an actual image of this healing begin to take place. I thank God over and over for this small, yet tangible evidence of His hand at work. You are sleeping peacefully and my hope is restored once again. A tear falls from the corner of your eye. I speak peace over you and ask angels to minister comfort and peace to your heart. I even ask them to sing to you. Even as I pray these quiet gifts over you, God also pours them out onto me.

Today is no exception as Donata pens a personal note to me which included a quote from Colossians 4:2. *"Devote yourselves to prayer; stay alert in it with thanksgiving."* The rest of the note read:

"Rest in My Presence, allowing me to take charge of this day. Do not bolt into the day like a racehorse suddenly released. Instead, walk purposefully with Me, letting Me direct your course one step at a time. Thank me for each blessing along the way. This brings joy to both you and to Me. A grateful heart protects you from negative thinking. Thankfulness enables you to see the abundance I shower upon you daily. Your prayers and petitions are winged into Heaven's throne room when they are permeated with thanksgiving. In everything give thanks, for this is My will for you. Devote yourselves to prayer, being watchful and thankful." Sarah Young – Jesus Calling

Tuesday, February 25th felt like a milestone when the nurse told me that while you had failed a breathing test, you had actually breathed partially on your own for twelve whole minutes for the first time since January 14th. You were awake when I came into your room and were even following simple commands while staying calm. You actually smiled when you saw me, a gift to this mother's heart. Fifteen visitors come this one day in the middle of the week. I am continually reminded how much you are loved.

The doctors explain that Lauren needs a feeding tube placed in her stomach to get that final tube out of her throat. Better nutrition should mean faster healing. I tell this to myself to offset my anxiety over being asked to sign yet another consent form for a procedure that carries substantial risks.

I panic when her blood pressure soars dangerously high, as I am so afraid of another stroke. After all, we haven't been able to get her awake enough to even know what damage has been sustained by the first stroke. It feels like another roller coaster day emotionally. We are reminded we have a long journey ahead. I was all too aware of that already.

I struggle when Lauren seems more sedated than this time last week. Her blank expressionless eyes make it hard to not fear a setback. It is terrible not knowing what is going on inside of her heart and mind. What will she remember? How will she cope with the stress once this is over? I have to believe this will be over one day. I think of those who live with Post Traumatic Stress Disorder, like soldiers returning from the battle field and women who survive domestic violence. *"Please heal her mind and her body, Lord."* I learn to know when she is stressed by the patterns in her breathing. Anxiety is not of the Lord, so I pray for His peace. His presence often brings that peace and calm right into the room.

Wednesday brings the procedure to insert the feeding tube, and more breathing tests. Lauren breathed on her own partially for three hours, then for another two hours. She passed the test. This is wonderful news. The doctor offers to show us the comparison x-rays and tells us what he is seeing is God's hand at work. It is comforting to have what you already know confirmed. It builds your faith.

A friend felt challenged to tell us that we should stop using the word critical and instead redeem its letters to declare that Lauren is:

C-hristian

R-emarkable

I-ntelligent

T-ough

I-nspiring

C-aring

A-ngel

L-auren

Perspective holds the power to alter an entire situation with such a small shift. I thank God for such a positive and beautiful reminder, and I also thank Him for giving us friends who are holding us up during this ordeal.

A simple bed bath causes your blood pressure to rise. The doctor reinforces that while you face a tremendous physical battle, you will also face emotional and spiritual mountains as you enter the rehabilitation phase of your recovery. Your dad decided that those of us waiting should be called the "patience" and those in the hospital room should just be called "sick" since we are the ones having to exercise our patience all the time. We got a good chuckle out of his vast medical wisdom, which was quite insightful and funny. I don't know what Lauren and I would have done without him.

Physical therapy is ordered. While this beginning of her rehabilitation feels like another milestone, her high blood pressure concerns me as to how much movement she will tolerate. I bring her favorite lip gloss and I can tell by her response that she smells and recognizes it. I love the idea of her having comforts from home.

The feeding tube is inserted, her vitals remain stable and another friend sends me another personalized devotion. God is supplying our needs in such a sweet and personal way. I am so grateful. It is becoming second nature to thank God continually. I find myself whispering: *"God, you are so good. How do we ever praise you enough for the good day Lauren has had? You and only You have her on the road to recovery. You are the Great Physician, the Healer, our Wonderful Savior, our Wonderful Friend, the Lord of Lords – how marvelous are Your ways. I thank you for blessing Lauren the way you are."*

Friday brings another good day. You are a bit more alert. I place lip gloss on your lips and you smile. I can tell you like that, as you even try to lift your head up off the pillow. I remind you that we have a beach trip ahead and you nod in agreement. It is wonderful to see even the slightest responses to know you are aware.

I promise the beach. Now, I find myself assuring you that when you get well, we will go again to your favorite city, New York, to buy pocket books. I know how to get you to respond. Sea, sun, sand and fashion … what gal wouldn't return to the land of the living for a little retail therapy?

Your dad and I continue to keep a bedside vigil and we often bungle over each other in your room. I know you are laughing inside as we obsessively remind each other to wash our hands and how to help you. How on earth did you become such a beautiful young lady with two loony parents like us? We call ourselves "Dumb and Dumber." We just never quite seem to agree on who is who!

You have a great nurse, another male nurse. I am so comforted when I feel peaceful about who is caring for you. Your dad continues to crack me up. He accuses me of hovering over you. He will often head out of the room, only hoping I will follow him. One time, when he got to the end of the hall, he turned around to see if I was following him. I started laughing so hard at his predictable behavior. I told him I was going to write this story down so you would know how funny he was being.

Today is the last day of February. You have been sick so long, but I am convinced you are getting better every day. I know you want to live as I watch you try so hard. I continue to pray and to celebrate what a fighter you have become – a beautiful and strong lady that I am proud to call my own daughter.

Today is Saturday and it marks the first of March when a benefit is being held for you at a local coffee shop where a co-worker and her husband are singing. You would love this! The nurses gave me a great report when I called this morning to check on you. Twenty eight people visit.

When I see you later that morning, you are making more eye contact and smiling a little bit. More medicine is reduced and I am hoping this will allow you to seem less expressionless and begin to really connect more. Until I bring your phone back in a few days, you begin to hear friends calling on my phone.

I thank God for the staff here who is most always in tune with trying new avenues to accomplish what they must in ways that allow Lauren to stay calm and peaceful.

Her dad tells me that he feels it would be just as effective if I would pray "Silently" at her bedside. He didn't want Lauren to realize the seriousness of her illness, fearing that would further upset her. I told him I wanted her to know I was there. We ended up laughing at how overprotective we both are as if Lauren were just a little girl. I know she will laugh to hear this story one day too. We may have expressed our presence differently, but the key was that we were both blessed to be present. We would not have had it any other way.

It is so hard to leave my daughter every night and return home. I often find myself sitting in my favorite chair thinking, if I am here in my chair, this can't be real. Then I realize it is really happening. I think chances are good we will all benefit from some therapy before this is over. Again, I can imagine you smiling at my thoughts.

I called in on my way to visit Sunday, March 2nd and got a good report. Even her blood pressure is stable today. Seeing her was wonderful. I can tell she wants to get out of bed and I take that as a good sign that she is becoming more alert. She tries hard to talk. The doctor says she is doing well. I ask if Lauren is out of danger. He replies that there is danger of infection as long as there are so many tubes invading her body. I choose to believe that Lauren is only moving forward now, not back. Physical therapy is finally ordered. Fifteen friends and family come to check on her and we learned that the coffee house benefit was a great success. The support and love are overwhelming.

I watch Lauren drift off to sleep multiple times throughout the day and I realize it shocks her every time she awakens to the sea of machines and people. This has to be confusing, and I try to reassure her that this is only temporary and that she is getting better every day.

Praying at her bedside comes easy under these circumstances. We have so much to be thankful for … small improvements, friends, family and caring staff. I choose yet another day to trust God's faithfulness even in the midst of what I cannot understand.

Monday marks another milestone. Lauren lasted six and a half hours on the breathing trial test. I arrive this day to a glorious surprise, Lauren sitting up in a chair by her bed. WOW! All I can do is praise God. Even thought it took a special hydraulic lift to get her out of bed because she is unable to walk, we are all jumping with joy at this simple accomplishment. She keeps trying to talk and ask questions. I cannot always understand her, but I find myself answering "yes" or "no." When it was not a yes/no question, she rolls her eyes at me. We all laugh! Wow, the simple joy of laughing and sitting up. Twenty people visit and share this milestone day.

It snowed and the nurse thought we should move her bed so she could watch. That simple act of kindness brought me so much joy. Lauren is emerging from a critical care patient back to simply being a person. Today, she made it seven hours on the breathing trial test. I can tell she is getting stronger, as her vitals stay stable during the move from bed to chair. By late afternoon, she was as tired as if she had done a full days' work. Her heart rate raced as evidence of her exhaustion. It begins to come down and I find myself thanking God for His faithfulness. I reminded myself and Lauren to stay anchored to that simple truth even when she doesn't understand all of what is happening. I cannot begin to imagine how frightening all of this is for her.

I sang for her today, but she didn't seem too thrilled. I can't imagine why. The doctor begins to discuss moving her back to Select Specialty Hospital and starting therapy. Today's overarching prayer is thanking God for giving wisdom to her caregivers in this complex situation.

Tuesday morning when I awoke, I felt like something was wrong. I asked God to forgive my lack of faith as I called to find Lauren had a restless night. It troubles me picturing her lying awake and "thinking." What is she thinking? Not being able to effectively communicate adds a great deal of heart ache to this ongoing situation.

For a day that began negative and anxious, it was about to turn positive. I arrive and she is off the ventilator being given liquid oxygen and breathing completely on her own for the first time since January 14th. The target was four hours if she could stay calm. The doctor is delighted and states that he wants to remove the central line soon, as it is a major risk of infection. He also says he feels she is almost ready to be evaluated for being permanently removed off the ventilator. He orders another MRI to evaluate the status of any damage to her brain.

I pray… *"Please God, let all evidence of that initial stroke on the first scan be gone on this one. You are able. All is well. We praise you for all you have done and are doing in Lauren's life. I am reminded that your Word promises you have plans for her life. This is awesome and exciting!"*

A friend sent a pillow that she made with Lauren's favorite M&Ms character on it … she mouthed, *"I love it."* Treasured friends have made this grueling journey possible.

Lauren is evaluated for returning to Select where there is hope of getting off of the ventilator. While there is much to be hopeful for, it grows frustrating as her efforts to talk more only leave us confused about what she is trying to tell us. She grows frustrated right along with us. Under any other circumstances, the amount of eye rolling and funny faces would have been quite amusing.

Frustration also continues over staff members who refuse to do simple things that could make her much more comfortable. She keeps saying her shoe is hurting her right foot, but she is not even wearing a shoe. We knew this was a sign of neuropathy, damage that had occurred to her nerves.

This new and odd behavior continues into Wednesday, March 3rd. Now I know this isn't just a quirky thing … something is bothering her about that right foot. She is complaining today that her right foot and hand are tingling. This makes me anxious about the upcoming report on her recent MRI. I have an anxious feeling about all of this. I quickly give my anxiety to God and ask Him to watch over her.

The scan confirmed a mild bleed into her brain which the doctor feels is what affected her left eye, causing a significant blind spot. He encourages us that if there was any other damage, it will be addressed in therapy and that the area appears to be healing now. He does not feel this is severe enough to require a neurologist to get involved. That is good news.

Plans are made to move her back to Select this afternoon, but her white blood cell count is up. That could mean an infection. Lauren received the news of the move well without anxiety. The move, on the other hand, did excite her. Her face was red and her heart raced. It took quite a while for her to calm down after getting into her new room.

My anxiety rises too because of the complications that developed last time she was here. She ended up being transferred back to ICU seriously ill. I'm having to really work on my own fear. I am reminded how far the Lord has brought Lauren and that His plans are to heal her and bring her out of this nightmare once and for all. I plead with God for the roller coaster ride to be over and for Him to please not let that start again. Leaving her that night was extremely hard, as she was in a new place with new, unknown anxieties.

I remind her as I leave that she is a strong, courageous, beautiful fighter. She shakes her head "no." I wish she could see the inner strength and beauty I see in her daily. I marvel that she is my daughter.

HEY, MOM!

I received a call this morning, Thursday March 6th, asking for consent to remove the central line and replace it with a less invasive type of line. Respiratory therapy placed a valve on her tracheotomy which allowed her voice to have a little bit of volume after months of silence. As I entered the room, to my surprise I heard, *"Hey Mom."* Thank you, God! It had been so long since I heard that sweet voice. We talked all afternoon until the nurse said *"Enough, she needs to rest!"* Before we were ordered to silence, Lauren brought up the pigs and butterflies she had lost and her need to be at the office by Friday. I realized the massive doses of medicines had created quite a barrage of hallucinations as she went on to describe our twin Volvos out in the parking lot. She was especially concerned that two dogs were in my car but had now been shot.

She also got to talk on the phone for the first time with two of her aunts. We even washed her hair and I lifted her arms so she could fluff her hair. I told the nurse that she has "magic fingers," a skill developed after almost twenty years as a cosmetologist.

Nineteen visitors also shared this victorious day.

I told Lauren about her co-workers raising money for her. The thought of their concern overwhelmed her. I explained that I would have to leave early today as the weather conditions included ice. She asked if she could go with me. I cannot wait until I can answer "yes" to that question.

Leaving was hard, as Lauren admitted that she didn't always feel she could trust the staff here. Once I am back home, a flood of emotions seemed to hit in waves. This still feels like almost more than I can bear.

When I arrive on Friday, March 7th, Lauren is sitting up in her recliner complaining about pain from a pressure sore. Physical therapy comes and helps her back to bed for a long nap. A scan of her liver shows nothing abnormal, which is a miracle after all of the medication that has been required to keep her alive.

I read some of her many cards to her and prayed at her bedside.

Saturday she was already sitting up when I arrived. I showed her a copy of the poster that hangs all over town advertising the benefit yard sale/cook out/bake sale scheduled for next weekend. We are both overwhelmed at the kindness of her co-workers who had coordinated this fund raiser. They even got Galaxy, a locally owned food market, to donate hot dogs for the event. That news, along with twenty visitors this one day, reminded us again that a loving community is indeed one of our best medicines at this stage in the journey.

Today, Lauren wanted to see her first visitors, my brother and his wife, who visited briefly at her request. This was another milestone for Lauren to feel well enough to begin connecting with family.

She continued to fabricate some funny stories. Today, she told us that Donata and Franklin Graham had purchased lots of shoes in different sizes so everyone could get the size they needed. We had to laugh.

Tonight, the time change shifts us forward an hour on the clock. That thought triggers a memory of all Lauren has missed... two major snow storms, an ice storm, the Super Bowl, Valentine's Day (not that she would mind missing that one). I look forward to Easter, the next major date on the calendar and pray all will be well by then. I thank the God of Easter for His unconditional love and provision during this time.

Lauren talked on the phone today with my other brother and his wife. It is such a joy to have friends and family who are just as excited as we are as this amazing daughter of mine gets stronger and stronger.

Sunday, Lauren stays off the ventilator for twenty hours. We are told that once she stays off for forty eight hours, the machine will be removed from the room. The complex combination of medicine she is receiving is still causing crazy thoughts. She worries more about the dogs being shot in my fictitious Volvo. I assure her we are looking for the people and they will be caught. I long for her to know what is real and what is not.

It's Monday and one staff member declares Lauren will likely remember this as "hell week" as therapy to get her moving begins. Due to the stroke and extended bed rest, her muscles were severely atrophied. To complicate her overall weakness, the stroke had weakened her entire left side. She would now begin the process of learning how to move and walk, much like a baby becoming a toddler.

The wound nurse leaves without ordering a new dressing for the pressure sore, which leaves Lauren in a lot of pain. The x-ray shows more fluid in the lungs that could lead to pneumonia. *"God, please protect her."*

Tuesday, March 11th brought an answer to that prayer. I walked in and the ventilator is GONE! Out of the room. The large tracheotomy tube was replaced by a smaller one, and it is valved so she can talk again. Therapy begins today and we are told she can begin eating real food after she passes the swallowing test.

Lauren asked to go back to bed as her pressure sore is causing severe pain. Her dad asks her if she can't sit up a bit longer since it is so good for her. She barks back, *"Stay out of it. I've got this."* Her inspiration for this quick quip was a framed get well card from her cousin and her husband that included the simple phrase, *"I've Got This."* We had a good laugh. It would appear that Lauren is back in charge and it's time for Mom and Dad to be silenced. We have hopefully made the last decisions and she is now at the helm.

Lauren's father was a tremendous support to us both throughout this entire ordeal. My gratitude, however, did not diminish my frustration. His obsessive compulsive behavior while in her room made me crazy as he tends to walk around, looking at all the machines, moving tubes around and asking questions I cannot answer about what needs to be done next. Wow, Lauren and I thought we were a bit obsessive compulsive. By comparison to him, we are laid back!

The therapist told me that you asked to be left in the lift that is used to get you from the bed to the chair, because when you are suspended in the sling, your pressure sore does not hurt. They explained they couldn't leave you hanging in mid air, as your mom wouldn't like that … they said you remarked, "Oh, she won't care."

Tonight, you told me you saw my father, your grandfather Parker standing behind me. Even though he is no longer alive, I am not going to question who or what you might see. After all the prayers of faith, it would not surprise me for God to allow you to see what others could not.

You asked me to get Heather on the phone so you could hear her sing with her angelic voice. A deep peace came over you during that call. We thanked God together for this treasured friend who has provided an ongoing spirit of worship throughout this entire ordeal.

Wednesday, Lauren is still worried about the fictitious cars. She asks me to move hers to her driveway and mine to my turn-a-round. She fears they might be vandalized here. I try to tell her not to worry, but she quickly reminds me of what happened to the "two dogs." I can't believe she remembers that dog story still. It must be so hard to have confusion merging with her reality. She quips that she needs a vacation to Gatlinburg, Tennessee. I assure her that I will take her as soon as she is able.

Time is wearing on me, as I find myself getting grumpy over seemingly small things. Her feet are so dry. I ask for someone to put lotion on them. No one can seem to agree on whose job that should be. Just another day in the hospital!

Lauren then gets focused on our upcoming Parker family picnic. She asks if her dad and Donata will be there. I remind her that they don't typically come to this event. She quickly remarked, *"Well, Dad thinks he is coming and if he comes, Donata should come also."* I told her that they were welcome and I reminded her that things have always been good between us. She seemed relieved that we were all getting along and how hard it would be for her if the dynamic was negative. I say out loud, *"Thank you, God, for the ability to be civil adults because we believe in You. Thank you for teaching us to love and value each other."*

It was hard to leave as Lauren's vitals were high due to such a busy day of activity and she had a hard time settling down to rest. On the way home, her dad reached toward the back seat of the car, took my hand and prayed for us all. My heart was filled with peace and joy at the thought of how much we both love our daughter and the joy of being able to be a united team on her behalf.

If we could share one message at this point, it would be to forgive and let go of the past. This paves the way for love and unity ahead ... we all knew that this was essential for Lauren's recovery.

Divorce does not hold the power to separate us. Love had built a bridge that would give Lauren access to each of us in this season. That realization blessed my heart over and over again. A nurse gave me a small note with Proverbs 20:24 on it: *"A man's steps are determined by the Lord..."*

This was a great reminder that Gods ways are always higher and better than our own. We choose to keep seeking His perfect path through this storm and we hold to faith that we will emerge as victors.

Two Months and Counting

"Waiting is often one of the greatest challenges God asks of us, but in the end, His timing is always perfect."
—*Betty Robinson*

Thursday, March 13th I arrived to Lauren laying flat with the TV on. I turned on the fan and opened the blinds to *"Let the sun shine in."* She smiled and seemed happy. It occurred to me that through this entire time, Lauren has NEVER COMPLAINED.

Coughing still elevates her heart rate. Oh, how I hope the new medicine will soon put an end to the endless cough. Lauren passed a swallowing test the first time, which the nurses said rarely ever happens. One step closer to a real meal ... she was about to receive crushed ice, thickened cranberry juice, applesauce, a graham cracker and milk as part of the testing. The food was all tinted blue so the scan could track the path as she swallowed, taking care to make sure no food was trickling into her lungs which could mean another bout of pneumonia.

Friday, she was allowed to order breakfast for the first time … grits, toast and apple juice. This felt like another milestone. When she would ask for something and it was not delivered quickly enough, I would get anxious and Lauren would remind me, *"Mom, just chill. They are really nice and they are trying."*

Her dad brought a gift today, a plaque that says, *"A lovely daughter."* She asked me to take it home so it would not get broken.

Lauren also asked today if she had a stroke after overhearing the therapist discussing her progress. We were honest and told her yes, but that she was blessed that it was mild enough that the neurologist could barely see it on the scans and he felt she would recover from it 100%. We took this opportunity to share some of the milestones of the past few weeks, details she had slept through. This was the remarkable timeline up to this point:

• JANUARY 12 – TAKEN TO THE EMERGENCY ROOM (ER) THEN SENT HOME WITH MEDICATION

• JANUARY 14 – RETURNED TO ER AND ADMITTED TO HOSPITAL IN HICKORY

• JANUARY 16 – TRANSFERRED TO ICU AND PLACED IN DRUG-INDUCED COMA AND COMPLETE PARALYSIS. PLACED ON VENTILATOR

• FEBRUARY 12 – TRACHEOTOMY INSERTED SURGICALLY

• FEBRUARY 18 – TRANSFERRED TO SELECT SPECIALTY HOSPITAL IN WINSTON SALEM

- FEBRUARY 21 – ADMITTED TO ICU AT FORSYTH IN WINSTON SALEM

- FEBRUARY 26 – SURGERY FOR FEEDING TUBE INSERTED IN HER STOMACH

- MARCH 5 – TRANSFERRED FROM ICU BACK TO SELECT

- MARCH 14 – HER FIRST MEAL SINCE JANUARY

That first meal was followed by Lauren brushing her own teeth and getting a bath that left her smelling like a model for Bath and Body Works. I am told that her old pressure sore is healing but now there is a new one. This concerns me as another strain on her body's healing mechanisms and another source for infection. Will this ever end?

Heather called to describe today's shopping outing that was not the same without Lauren. Lauren gave her instructions on what to buy for her and that I would come to pick up the clothes. I could not wait until she could shop and wear real clothes.

Lunch time comes and she enjoyed turkey, gravy and vegetables, even dessert. It is so wonderful for me to watch her enjoy eating, such simple pleasures.

As Lauren was relaxing, her dad tried to fix her pillow and she remarked, *"Why do you have to keep mashing down on my head?"* She later realized he was praying for her.

She rested well this afternoon. I am so thankful because I know how important sleep is to her recovery.

Today was the first day of the benefit yard sale. Her co-worker Steve dressed in a dog costume and pleaded for folks to come in… and come in they did. What a success! What a treasure to have such amazing friends.

Saturday, March 15th I stopped by Lauren's home to get her mail, let her car run and turn off the heat. I stopped by the yard sale to offer my thanks and support. Sales were already greater than what was expected.

Lauren was having a good day when I arrived with goodies and snacks from the yard sale for us to enjoy. Her dad washed her hair while the CNA fixed a nice, clean bed. Lauren was now focused on wanting a real bath, saying she would probably have to go to a hotel to get one.

Once again, the staff tells us almost daily stories of individuals dying from complications related to H1N1 flu. I pen these words of gratitude in my journal this particular day, to Lauren and to God:

Lauren, when I think about what you have overcome, I am just amazed! You are a miracle – there's no other name for it. God has blessed you in a mighty way. He has such a wonderful work for you to share – all He ever wants us to do is tell others about Him and praise Him. I know you will have plenty of opportunities. Your days ahead are going to be so exciting to see who He puts in your path. I know your future will be God-centered. He has chosen you for something special. You are gifted in your way with people. That's why you have so many friends. You have the ability to touch many lives and I know Jesus is going to bring much good from this season. How exciting!

Thank you, God, for allowing me to be Lauren's mother. I am so honored! Even if I had not been her mother, what a joy it would be to call her friend. I feel now as if I possess a double blessing of being her mother and her friend.

I'VE GOT THIS

Sunday, March 16th, the staff forgot her breakfast. Lauren quickly said it was because "Mom" wasn't there. Once an early lunch arrived, Lauren began feeding herself for the first time. She continued to declare her new motto. *"I've got this."*

Monday began with a drive to Winston Salem peppered with sleet and another forgotten breakfast. Actually, I went on to learn that it wasn't forgotten but that her oxygen levels had dropped too low and the staff was busy trying to trouble shoot the situation. By the time lunch arrived, she was hungry but almost too weak to feed herself. I had to leave early due to the weather, but it worked out well since all Lauren really wanted was to nap. Eleven people braved the bad weather to visit.

Seeing Lauren take her medicine by mouth for the first time and receiving a surprise Hershey bar from her dad made this hard day a bit better for me. Chocolate should probably be prescribed to patients for its many medicinal benefits! It certainly did get me through a few tough days.

Tuesday marked a few milestones, including graduating from pureed to real food and physical therapy in the gym instead of the room. Lauren actually remarked to the doctor how much she enjoyed therapy.

During a breathing treatment, the speaking valve is in place so we can hear her voice more clearly. It sounds so strong and we can understand her completely. I am reminded yet again that the Lord is in charge, as the staff had said her voice would be extremely weak and she would most likely need therapy to regain strength and volume. Evidently, the doctors are not aware of who is REALLY in charge of her recovery. Thank you, precious Lord, for preserving her voice. We all laughed as she picked on her dad for packing his own lunch today. We could understand every word she said!

On her way to physical therapy, I heard her in the hall telling everyone "Hello" – back in the real world. I told her to go ahead and wave at them all as if she is a princess in a parade. You can tell I'm the proud mom.

Even in the midst of these simple joys, our hope is challenged as Lauren began having severe leg pain as her activity increased. She tries to call for help or medicine, but the staff cannot hear her because her nurse call button was broken. What do individuals without an advocate do in situations like this? I am so thankful we have each other.

We were so exhausted coming home that we drove right past one of our parked cars and had to return once we remembered where it was parked.

Wednesday, March 19th marks another breathing trial test. It will require forty-eight hours before Lauren's tracheotomy can come out permanently. She even helped give herself the breathing treatment and test. One of her ICU doctors was on the floor today and stopped by to say hi and check on her. The doctor said she will have a story to tell, but not anytime soon. He said it may be like a soldier with Post Traumatic Stress Disorder. It may take a while before she is ready to "re-live" the ordeal. Fifteen people visited. Lauren begins to ask for her computer and phone, but we feel it is a bit early. Our friend Heather sent pictures of many of Lauren's friends for her to enjoy.

A pain specialist comes to see Lauren regarding her leg pain. He confirms that she has nerve damage and proposes to change her medicine. He seemed hopeful that it will improve as her activity level increases. Small tasks still cause anxiety. This is hard to watch, especially as Lauren has to work to stay calm during simple daily tasks while the breathing test continues. It is times like this that remind me how far Lauren still has to go to recover, as the simplest of activities cause her breathing to be erratic and her vitals to soar. I tried to calm her down before leaving … this type of day makes leaving her unimaginably hard.

Thursday, March 20th is the first day of spring. I thank God for the fragrance of new life and the hope of a new season. I distinctly remember this time last year, celebrating Lauren's good results after a questionable mammogram led to an ultra sound. Here we are in a bit larger test, which could only mean one thing to women of faith … we will have even more to celebrate!

Lauren is still accumulating hours toward the forty-eight hour goal of her breathing test. She has to make it until 1:30 tomorrow. Her dad and Wayne become physical therapy coaches, exercising with her a lot. Then her dad washed her hair. It sure has been convenient having a barber in the family. Thirteen people visited and Lauren even got to talk with a couple of friends on the phone. Sarah was so overcome that she cried. I heard Lauren ask if she needed to borrow her oxygen. She then called and joked around with Teresa, telling her she was stupid in their funny, sisterly banter. I know that made Sarah and Teresa's day. It is such a joy to see Lauren begin to reconnect and have the energy to reach beyond her day to day survival, even if the reach is still somewhat shortened.

Friday, March 21st marked a major milestone, removal of the breathing tube. The doctors had to explain the risks and get consent. Little do they know, but we know who is really in charge. It is God, not them. I love seeing our faith collectively grow in the midst of this crazy journey to the point where we begin to thank God and turn to God as our first response, not simply as a reaction when crisis comes. It is a joy to see Lauren head to the gym for therapy in her recliner after the procedure. A hole in her throat was not going to be enough to stop her today.

She returned from the gym exhausted and shivering cold to the point that her teeth were chattering. We got blankets to warm her and she drifted off to sleep for a while, then "stuff" started to happen. Her heart rate soared upward as her oxygen levels dropped downward. Teresa and Sarah had come to visit, but were only allowed to stay a few short minutes.

The doctors began to discuss treatment options. One felt the tracheotomy came out too soon and should be reinserted. One wanted to wait and see, ordering extreme rest in the meanwhile. They went with the later decision, thank God! I stayed the night to keep her calm and to reassure her that all was going to be OK. We got through the night with the multiple interruptions of sleep that occur in the hospital;

pills, nursing checks, vitals, etc. Lauren needs rest more than ever, but this is an exhausting setting to be in.

Saturday, the doctors decide her elevated heart rate is partly due to dehydration, so we make plans to police her to get more liquid during the day. We spent the day resting, reading cards and Facebook posts and thanking God for a peaceful day. The love of her friends and family made us all cry. Lauren got a good laugh out of the fact that I get as excited as she does when she hears from her friends.

Today, the doctor declared he wants to get Lauren out of here before the hospital makes her sick. I begin to envision: rehabilitation, home, then our trip to the beach. I love getting small glimpses of life after the hospital.

Two sweet ladies from the food service department stopped by to take Lauren's order for dinner tonight. I joked that this was like a five-star hotel. I am quite certain the bill will reflect the star level. I marvel that the throat wound has almost closed in just a day and I take a moment to thank God for no infection.

Sunday, March 23rd, the charge nurse overheard a CNA being verbally abusive to Lauren when she was alone. The nurse quickly intervened and told the CNA to leave the room and never return. My heart continues to break as Lauren's illness is enough to deal with in and of itself. These other challenges threaten to push my heart over the edge.

Monday, we were thankful for a quiet and uneventful day of therapy, resting and visiting together.

Tuesday, she was already in therapy when I arrived. Therapy is helping her leg pain and today she was able to place her feet flat on the floor for one of the first times. She even used light weights during arm exercises. This is all being done to prepare her for more intense rehabilitation. She will have to tolerate several hours of therapy a day in order to be moved to this next type of facility.

Today brought another great moment, as Lauren was able to conference by phone with her work family at MDI in Hickory, North Carolina. This call didn't just make her a little happy. I saw her million-dollar smile for the first time. This same group had gathered early on in their conference room to pray for Lauren.

Sixteen other friends also stopped by to encourage Lauren … I wish she had the energy to visit with each person face to face. I have to believe that will come in time.

By Wednesday, an infection had Lauren on another strong antibiotic. Lauren was turned down at the rehabilitation center of our choice because she was unable to walk. The goal now will be building her endurance so she can qualify. Her new wheelchair came today and I was surprised that her response was one of excitement and gratitude. I continue to marvel at her attitude and faith. My prayers today focus on thanking God for her amazing outlook and hope.

Another tube, the PICC line was removed, getting her one step closer to being transferred out of here. The doctors evaluate her complaints of more numbness and odd sensations in her right fingers and over her stomach. They agree this is coming from her nerves healing. She did manage to lift her arms and legs at the same time, causing me to marvel at the strength she is gaining.

Thursday, March 27th, the doctors are still busy searching for a rehab facility that will admit Lauren at her low level of mobility and endurance. Early that morning Lauren had been transferred into her wheelchair, only to quickly realize that plastic had been left on the new seat cover, causing her to almost slide out of the chair. She began crying and calling for help. A doctor who was passing by came to her rescue. This was a clear picture of how fragile she still was at this stage, unable to even catch herself as she began falling from her chair.

Later after calming down, Lauren decided to nap in order to feel rested up for a visit with Heather and Julie. Fifteen people came by today to encourage us. One memory that stands out is one of her respiratory therapists remarking that she should write a book because she has a story people will want to hear.

It feels as if the insurance and case managers are calling all the shots on where Lauren will go next for rehab, causing me to feel anxiety at the thought of her not having the high tech equipment that monitors her breathing status. I know that we will need God's timing and His protection in this next phase of her recovery.

Lauren asked at one point if we were by ourselves. I told her yes. She asked why her dad kept going out of the room and putting on more cologne every time he would come back in. We had a good laugh over his smoking habit that he was trying to "cover." I broke into a much-need uncontrollable laugh and immediately felt the stress of the day begin to fade away. Lauren and I both laughed in a good-hearted way over her father who had been ever present throughout this journey. It was good to be able to laugh together about our unique family dynamic.

THE FRESH PRINCESS OF BELAIRE

Friday came and we learned it would be her day to transfer to rehab. She would be going to a facility in Gastonia, North Carolina called Belaire Health Care. She immediately quipped, *"I guess that makes me the fresh princess of Belaire."* I marveled at her attitude and sense of humor. I begin to get more vision, daring to hope that she will walk again soon.

Lauren arrived there safely around 8:00 pm. I prayed, specifically thanking God for the staff at Select that contributed to her recovery to this point. I decided to spend the night since it had been a traumatic day of transition. The EMS staff had dropped her hard onto the stretcher and had bruised her back. She has been through so much. At times, I feel that one more small oversight or setback could push my heart over the edge into despair. She does not deserve to suffer more.

We end the day reading her cards. One held the message reminding Lauren how easy it would be to question God as to why this was all happening, but to hold out hope that He will continue to reveal His character and that He makes no mistakes. We became emotional and thanked God for sustaining her and loving us unconditionally. The fourteen friends who shared this day with us were a tangible reminder of His great love.

Saturday, March 29th began at 1:00 am when staff came in to assess her. Can you believe that? I was furious. The bandage was changed on her pressure sore to a new flexible style that moved as she moved. I immediately wondered why this wasn't used at Select, as the rigid bandage pulled her skin, causing constant pain.

Physical therapy staff came in the morning and assisted Lauren to sit up on the side of her bed. She was almost able to do this alone with their coaching and supervision. This simple accomplishment was such a wonderful sight.

The new doctor came by to meet her. We liked him immediately, as he had a warm and caring demeanor. That put our hearts at ease.

I spent the night again. We laughed, prayed and marveled that twenty-four people had stopped by today to mark her first full day as the fresh princess of Belaire.

At 4:00 am, Lauren was having trouble breathing and she desperately needed the assistance of the nursing staff. They were nowhere to be found. This led to a huge confrontation when I realized that no one had been in Lauren's room for over five hours. What if I had not stayed? Her oxygen had dropped to a dangerously low 75 and she had become anxious.

I asked for the nursing supervisor's phone number, but the nurse on duty would not give it to me. I blasted her and threatened to call her supervisor. Eventually, another nurse got involved after I finally got the supervisor's number and called myself. She was hesitant, as she lived two hours away. Hearing the concern in my voice, she finally agreed to come and intervene.

As the situation unfolded, it became clear that Lauren

had not been given her midnight breathing treatment, leading to the drop in her oxygen levels, a potentially life-threatening situation. Mama lion reminded the staff that I was free to call the police force to report negligence, as Lauren was entrusted to their care. A family meeting was set for the next day. The nurse reported that I had screamed at her and threatened her. I assured her I was about to scream right now at the accusations and excuses that kept mounting to cover a simple case of negligence that could have placed my daughter at risk. The nurse would never say why she had failed to go into Lauren's room but the CNA went on to say that she had been instructed to not disturb the patient in room 14.

I demanded to get to the bottom of who had "ordered" for no one to enter the room. No one would accept responsibility, as they all seemed to simply be verbally covering for each other. The CNA finally apologized. The nurse did not. Another meeting was to be scheduled with the facility administrator. I was not comforted. How was I to feel secure leaving Lauren here?

The same day, her pain medicine was given five hours late. Testing showed her bladder infection was getting worse. The doctor did take quick action to resolve this issue. So far, this transfer was feeling like another nightmare.

I have a home to check on, a job I now often go to after midnight, but I knew I could not leave Lauren here alone. Lauren pressed her nurse call button. Twelve minutes passed. What if she couldn't breathe or what if she was sliding out of her chair again? The shift change came and went with no nurse in sight. The nurse finally came in late with her pain medicine and challenged me to "Just be patient." She checked lines and tubes, then left the room abruptly while mumbling something under her breath.

I was thankful to have a friend relieve me so I could go catch up on work during the day and have an emotional break from this nightmare.

The doctor set up a schedule where the CNAs have to check her oxygen levels and log them every fifteen minutes. They go the extra step to wake me every time to report their findings. It baffles me that it always seems to take me being pushed to my breaking point for Lauren to simply get the care she needs based on the complexity of her health crisis.

We were grateful for the therapy staff really pushing Lauren to her limits physically. She was now able to get onto her side, prop on her elbow and push herself up to a sitting position. I petition God to bring on the day quickly when she can walk out of this place. Seventeen people join our army of ongoing encouragement by stopping by today. A local retailer even sent a huge M&M display. That made her day.

I grow concerned as the nights seem to be marked by her oxygen levels dropping and her heart rate increasing. I know her body is under some kind of attack. What is going on, God? I find myself crying out to God to not let anything happen to her at this stage when she has come so far.

I pray: *"Lord, I cannot imagine what Lauren is going through and what her thoughts and feelings are. But you know, so Lord I ask you to keep her calm. Give her your sweet peace and let her feel your love every minute. God, we could not get through this without you. You are all we have and all we need."*

I find myself needing God as much as Lauren does at this point, as my heart-breaking mood feels that it will overtake me. God provided just the right friend to call me the next day as I was driving to be with Lauren. She encouraged me to pour out my heart and cry if needed. That release got my heart ready for another day. We were reminded of the challenge offered by one of her nurses in Winston Salem at Select when Lauren was discharged. She had simply reminded Lauren that there would be good days and bad days, but to expect the good to begin to outnumber the bad. We tried hard to hold onto this hope!

Wednesday, April 2nd started off rough. Lauren actually got sick and vomited after breakfast. She did therapy even while feeling this sick and her oxygen levels suffered afterward. It broke my heart when she told me how much she wished she was not here.

I sit by her bed, watching her fall asleep. I rub her feet and watch her oxygen levels with the intensity of the night watchman. I think about how she still cannot stand a shoe on her foot. The ongoing pain and low oxygen levels worry me. I quietly whisper, *"Lord, this is all in your hands. Please have mercy on Lauren."* She smiles while she sleeps and I know the Lord is answering by giving her His peace.

GOD BLEW ME A KISS

Thursday, I received the most wonderful phone call of my life. *"Hey, Mom. You won't believe where I am. I'm in my wheelchair and I'm outside. I've got on real clothes and shoes and I just stood up three times for ten seconds each time."* She went on to try and explain the wave of emotions – fear, excitement, happiness – all washing over her at once. She remarked how she had always taken the soft breeze and the song of the birds for granted. She said the wind on her face felt like God blowing her a kiss.

Her friends call to congratulate her. She smiles as big as I have ever seen her smile today. This is like medicine for my own heart too! Sixteen more friends stop by to remind her how loved she is.

Lauren even commands the praises of the staff today. We give thanks to God, praising Him for what He did for her today. I thanked Him for His love, His promises, His comfort, His peace and His joy. Those life-lines were all orchestrated by Him and we were increasingly aware that we could not make it without His sustaining grace. Even Lauren's attitude of *"I can do this"* was God sent.

I always look forward to quiet evenings alone when we can talk and I can try to find small ways to make her feel better. We make plans for her to come home with me for a while after she is discharged from rehab. How will I ever let go of this protective role I have been thrust into? I know that will be a challenging transition for my heart.

Friday, April 4th is a good day in therapy. Friends plan to visit later today and Sarah offered to spend the night. I agree, reluctantly, to stay home tonight. Letting go was as hard as if Lauren were a little girl again. My heart is with Lauren, so I am most comfortable when I am right there with her. I had to make myself leave.

I got stopped by the police on my drive home, as I had

turned left on a red light. I didn't admit that I had done it on purpose. Sitting through another light meant three more minutes I had to stay awake. He offered to give me a ticket or a sermon – I wisely chose the sermon, and boy, was I relieved! I shared what had been going on and he said he would pray for Lauren. I chuckle at the Lord using my traffic stop in order to grow Lauren's prayer warrior army.

My single night home was productive and I was thankful for Sarah. I did laundry and got a good night's rest. I know the break was good for Lauren too, although that was a bit hard for me to admit. I arrived to find a tired Sarah who had stayed awake and on call most of the night watching out for her "bestie." The awareness of how tired she was after staying one night reminded me that God really was giving me supernatural endurance beyond anything that could make sense to my natural mind.

Lauren admits that she loves the end of the day when we get to quietly visit and pray. A peaceful calm comes over her room. A kind nurse gets a larger oxygen monitor to make it easier for this night watchman to monitor her levels during her sleep.

Sunday, we had the kind of dinner you would expect to enjoy at Grandma's house after church in the South. Donata brought home-cooked chicken pie, green beans, rolls and brownies. It was so delicious!

Lauren was trying hard to reduce the amount of pain medication she was taking. The real risk of a drug addiction in situations like this was a reality we had been warned about, but I could not even let myself go there. I ask God to help her in this transition. Her attempts at reducing pain medication seem to be premature, as she is in excruciating pain that is making it impossible for her to sleep.

I watch Lauren endure countless setbacks and hurdles, all with her attitude of perseverance. I am blessed and challenged by her heart. I thank God for her full recovery, as I choose to believe this will be the outcome eventually.

A happy phone call made Lauren's heart rate go up, she assured me it was in a *good way*. I thank God for her friends and our family.

Monday, April 7th, I visited one of her original doctors in Hickory, NC. He reminded me that ARDS heals slowly, but he did believe her lungs would completely recover in time. I needed that encouragement in this season where the progress seems to have slowed and the days grew long and stressful.

Meanwhile, back at Belaire, another nurse forgot her breathing treatment again and her oxygen level dropped from 93 to 63. I ran to get the nurse. She came in and declared it was 93, not 63. I had to point out that she was reading the monitor upside-down. How could this be happening? I have no medical training and yet I am catching all of these critical mistakes that could cost Lauren her life. The nurse went screaming out of the room, calling for another nurse over the intercom. Her attitude and her incompetence startled me. Here we go again.

Lauren reminds me later about the respiratory therapist in Winston Salem who had remarked she should write a book. Some days, Lauren felt her story could be a comedy and days like today would make it an intense thriller full of drama and trauma. She actually seemed serious about turning this grueling story into a book. She even had a possible title: *"God's Got This."* I ask God to guide Lauren and make a way if it is His will for her story to be shared with others on the other side of this unimaginable journey. At this stage, fear gripped my heart at the thought of what it would take emotionally for Lauren to have to relive the story in order to tell it. Mama lion never rests!

I know she is alright on some level, as today she is craving her favorite sandwich from one of her favorite restaurants. She and I prayed, with Lauren focused on the realization that God has His hand on her life. She notes how this is changing her relationship with Jesus and I pray asking God to direct His perfect plan for her life.

For the next couple of days, I pay close attention as Lauren's left eye does not seem normal. Her pupil seems less reactive to light. I pray begging God to not let her have another stroke or setback of any kind.

Tuesday, Lauren had a good day in therapy but was struggling with leg pain. I rubbed them and she said this gave her some comfort. Tonight, as I prayed, Lauren also prayed aloud, thanking God for sustaining her and knowing her needs as she is relying totally on Him. She also thanked the Lord for her parents and prayed for us to be strengthened and blessed. That's my daughter, focusing on others even in a situation like this. I am so thankful to have a daughter who is full of faith. I logged fifteen faithful visitors as the day drew to a close.

Wednesday, April 9th was a dreaded day, as a meeting was scheduled to discuss the crisis and neglect that occurred this past Monday night. I asked God to communicate for me and to be my advocate, as I struggle to know how to advocate for Lauren. Her safety and recovery has to be my top priority and yet I desire to operate in a spirit of unity and love.

The meeting went well, directed by the administrator who assured us that her safety was his top concern. He welcomed our concerns and suggestions as to how they could care for Lauren better. As I was allowed to speak, he took meticulous notes and assured me that each issue would be addressed. I felt somewhat reassured but still left the meeting with the overwhelming weight of how each patient today is only safe if they have an advocate twenty-four hours a day, as negligence and incompetence complicate medical care.

We also had a meeting the same day with the therapy staff for an update on her progress. The staff is amazing and assured us they felt the same about her progress.

A day of meetings and stress ended quietly sitting outside enjoying the sun and then coming into the dining hall to hear a staff member sing.

Our favorite nurse here came to say goodbye, as he was headed to the beach for a week. This made my heart long for the day when that would be Lauren and me waving goodbye to the cares of the world for a coastal get-away. I had faith that our turn would come.

Our prayer time was full of gratitude for God going before us in all aspects of this day and continuing to direct her recovery. I am more aware than ever that the outcome is in His hands completely, as we would not have it any other way.

Lauren was surprised Thursday to receive a personal apology from the nurse who had forgotten the breathing treatment, setting off the course of events that led to yesterday's meeting. I never received an apology but this was enough for me, as Lauren is the one here who matters most. My heart was relieved.

A signature might seem like a small thing, but it felt huge today as Lauren was able to sign a consent form for some medication to be left in her room. These small steps feel huge to us right now, as Lauren continues to take the reins back on her own life. Lord, help me know how and when to let go.

Wayne, Lum and I decided finally to start a night rotation here so I could get more rest and no one would get more tired than necessary. I actually headed home for the first time in a long while. As I drove home, I marveled that I again logged seventeen people who came by today to check on our sweet girl. The outpouring of love continues to amaze and sustain me.

Friday and Saturday lingered on slowly, but Sunday brought an unexpected and worrisome change. Lauren awoke sick on her stomach. She settled down somewhat later in the morning, but got sick again while trying to eat lunch outside. I hoped it was due to the food we brought to her last night simply being too rich for her fragile system. I grow more concerned as I watch her oxygen levels drop more as she struggles.

I was so thankful that I would be spending the night. She was slightly better the next day, able to eat a bit while taking medicine for nausea. I feared that while her rehabilitation needs were being met here, her medical needs were not. Mama lion requested for pulmonary doctors to be called in to evaluate her status. I began to feel that this move had been premature and that she may not have been medically ready for rehab.

My worst fear became reality when the doctor confirmed that Lauren had double pneumonia AGAIN. How could this be happening? How could she endure the devastation to her body?

I took immediate action, advocating for her to be moved where her lung condition could be properly addressed and treated. The nurse on call was compassionate and informative, putting Lauren at ease. She even asked for us to call her later after her shift with an update on her personal phone.

Tuesday, April 15th, Lauren was transferred by ambulance to Carolina's Medical Center (CMC) back to the Intensive Care Unit (ICU). She was diagnosed with pneumonia and dehydration. The staff wasted no time collecting key information and getting her care underway.

I had to admit to God that I did not understand why He would allow this setback, but I was choosing to trust Him completely. My prayers focused on pleading with Him to keep Lauren encouraged and free from depression. I knew we had to keep her fighting.

At first, they limited her food intake in case she had to go back on a ventilator. Again, I begged God to keep this from happening. Praise God, she continued to breathe on her own! That was a huge victory.

I became more aware at this stage how responsible Lauren feels for everyone else and their needs. I encourage her that now is a time for her to put herself first in order to focus on getting well. How had I managed to not notice how much she strives to please people even at her own expense? I pray asking God to free her from the burden of trying to care for others while she is so sick.

I am immediately aware that this is the first facility where I have not felt that I had to tell people how to do their jobs. Her care is magnificent and a mother's heart is finally able to rest.

I spoke with a case manager from the insurance company who was sensitive to the fact that we did not feel Lauren's complex medical situation made her a good fit for Belaire and that when the time comes for her to resume rehabilitation, we would prefer a different facility. We needed a place that combined excellent therapy with the medical expertise to deal with her pulmonary complications. Those facilities would be few and far between.

Lauren was able to eat a bit of dinner and I thanked God that she is breathing on her own, maintaining descent oxygen levels. I asked Him to turn this pneumonia around quickly with no lasting setback. She was coughing constantly and couldn't seem to get warm.

The doctors and nurses worked to secure the best combination of medications and the best way to deliver the supplemental oxygen she needs. Lauren assures me she will not give up. I find myself praying constantly at this stage, trusting God to turn this around and to keep my precious daughter encouraged.

The staff was constantly checking in on her to assess her needs and oxygen levels. This is such a relief to know she is in such competent hands.

Wednesday, the doctor wanted to test Lauren to see if she had developed a chronic infection in her bronchial tube from the tracheotomy and ventilator use over time. He was shocked this had not already been done.

AM I GOING TO DIE?

I could tell her body was struggling as she was now sleeping most of the time. When she did wake for a short time, she said she was afraid she was going to die. My heart was crushed to know how much fear and anxiety were gripping her heart. I prayed asking God to give her His peace, as fear is not from Him. We had a discussion about death and eternity. We agreed that the most important thing is for a person to know they are at peace with God and ready for Him to receive their spirit if death did come. I really struggled having this discussion with my daughter who was young and healthy until just months ago.

Corrie Ten Boom, Holocaust Survivor and Protector of Persecuted Jews, once said: *"Hold everything in your hands lightly, otherwise it hurts when God pries your fingers open."* I knew I had to hold Lauren lightly at this stage in the journey, as once again, the future now loomed overwhelmingly uncertain. I may be Mama lion, but the Lord is the Lion of Judah and I knew He would have the final word on her destiny.

Thursday, the pulmonary doctor visited and remarked how amazed he is that Lauren's mind is so sharp after needing oxygen so long. He assured us that this bout of pneumonia will not worsen her ARDS or further damage her lungs. What a relief! The doctor orders for her therapy to continue so she won't lose ground on the progress she has made.

Lauren is finally moved out of ICU into a regular room with less sophisticated monitoring equipment. I find my own anxiety increasing when I cannot visually keep up with the numbers that we have learned how to read. My faith is getting taken to another level as I now have to fully rely on God to escort her out of this valley of death.

I am so tired of having to fill new staff members in on every detail each time she is transferred to a new room or a new facility. The new room is tiny, certainly not a five-star hotel like she requested.

Lauren was so exhausted that she fell asleep during our prayer time, only to awake wanting to have another prayer time. At this stage, more prayer is better, so we prayed again.

Saturday, Lauren seemed a bit stronger. We grow concerned as certain types of pneumonia are ruled out, leaving the doctors a bit puzzled as to what is causing all of this. They mention something attacking her immune system. I immediately ask the Lord to allow them to discover a treatable situation and to turn this around quickly.

I worried that Lauren was starting to hallucinate again, as she exclaimed she saw a white kitten. Turns out it was just my white hair passing in front of her mirror due to the distortion in her vision. If it wasn't white before, it sure was white now. We had a good laugh. Proverbs 16:31 says: *"Gray hair is a crown of glory; it is gained by living a godly life."* (NLT) Some Bible translations say it is a crown of wisdom. Either way, glory or wisdom, I could only pray that my physical appearance would one day reflect the deep work this journey was accomplishing in my heart.

Sunday, April 20th is Easter Sunday. *"Thank you, God, for this glorious day. Thank you for the gift of your Son and for His glorious resurrection."* I realize that the power of the resurrection had never felt as anointed as it did for us this year. It is amazing how a posture of vulnerability will cause you to realize on a new level how dependent we are daily on God continuing to resurrect us, thus giving us life, strength and purpose. I have a sense that this will be an Easter I will always remember!

The doctor mentioned a potentially serious condition as one possible cause of this recent setback, but today, I place my full faith in the life-giving power of a God who was resurrected from the dead in order to make life possible for me … and my daughter. If He could be resurrected from the dead, He could certainly resurrect her from the threat of death. Thirteen people made Lauren part of their Easter, stopping by to share their love.

I am so aware of how the Lord has protected Wayne, Lauren's dad and me as we have stayed healthy while also being with Lauren twenty-four hours a day and constantly coming and going from the hospital. The Lord knew she needed us and He sustained us for this time. Our ability to stay well while "living" in an environment that contained every known contagious germ was a miracle in and of itself. For this, we praised His holy name.

Lauren was being shuffled around with a new room two days in a row. This always causes me concern as she is so fragile. I learned about a person at CMC who was willing to help us. He sent food vouchers, parking passes and said he would do everything possible to help get Lauren into their rehabilitation facility when she is ready. I knew God had gone before us and was showing favor to Lauren. I cannot explain what it felt like to know someone in this high position was on our side. As I was advocating for Lauren, God was advocating for me! For us!

While now off of her antibiotics, the cause of Lauren's recent issues was still a mystery. A large team of specialists was assembled to problem solve. Her newest room is huge with hardwood floors and a pull out bed. We may never know for sure, but her new accommodations felt like the behind-the-scenes work of our "new friend." I thanked God then and there as every improvement, whether in her health or the details surrounding her care, were all ultimately from Jesus. Shortly after thanking God, our friend paid Lauren a personal visit. He left his card and assured us we could call if we needed anything. We again petitioned for her to be accepted to CMC's rehab facility. I expressed that I would feel confident she would be receiving the best care there. He nodded in agreement and quietly left her room. The favor we felt washed over us like a refreshing waterfall.

As positive as the day had been, we still ended up talking that night about our desires if one should die before the other. I had to admit there was still a possibility that Lauren could die, but I could not linger there long as my heart could not bear to imagine life without her. We were always close, but the bond between us had grown immeasurably since she became so sick. My heart returned to an email Lauren had sent back in November for my birthday which highlighted the special relationship shared by mother and daughter. It was precious and true.

Wednesday, April 23rd, Lauren received a visit from nursing students who had been at Belaire. We told them that we were praying she would be accepted at CMC's rehab facility so she could continue to receive the medical care required by her fragile lungs. Lauren also received a visit from a representative from the rehab center, explaining how the transition would work if she was approved.

Lauren became anxious after seeing a television report of patients being abused by staff in rehab facilities across the nation. While I am so thankful that she is honest with me, the weight of the worry she is carrying also breaks my heart. I remind God that I know He has a unique and specific purpose for Lauren's life.

Thursday, the hardest person to please was delighted with her progress in therapy. Lauren actually pleased herself! She stood up with a walker multiple times beside her bed.

I reactivated her cell phone as a celebration. Her day got even better at the news that she had now lost forty-seven pounds. She feels hopeful that her body is headed toward becoming healthy once again.

Fifteen people were logged on her guest list this day

alone. The amazing outpouring of love and support seemed almost endless.

Saturday, the doctors remain confused on why this recent setback occurred. They mention possibly needing to do a painful bone marrow biopsy. I pray this will not be needed, as she has been through so much. We choose to do something fun and distracting, so I paint her toenails "Hot Tamale" orange. Those flashy nails inside of her new orange tennis shoes should prepare her to attack rehab with style. Now, if only she could be accepted.

FINDING LIGHT IN THE TUNNEL

CHAPTER 6

*"God has made beauty
in the midst of brokenness."*
— *Shannon Dingle*

Finally, on Monday, April 28th, the hematologist says he feels that her white blood cell count is high due to all that her body has been through. Instead of more painful testing, he opted to retest her in three months. We were relieved! This good news meant she could be launched into the next chapter of her ongoing journey ... rehabilitation at CMC. Her acceptance came and we rejoiced. Lauren tells this next story best...

Today, I was moved to rehab by an actual underground tunnel that connected the hospital to the rehabilitation center. To this day, I still refer to this as my "tunnel of change." This image burned into my memory so strong that it became the inspiration for my book cover, as it represents going into a dark place of uncertainty only to emerge victoriously into the light. As I entered into rehabilitation for the second time, I was well aware that I had a long road ahead of me. But that was the beauty of it all ... I did have a road ahead of me and I could begin to see a glimmer of hope. If my initial admission to the hospital and the severe illness that gripped my body could be compared to going into a dark tunnel, this was more like seeing light at the end of a long grueling journey.

The season I was in the coma was like one long dark night. I have a frightening convergence of clear memories mingled with haunting hallucinations. For weeks, the distorted combination of truth and fiction left me feeling so buried by the dark that I began to wonder if this day would ever come ... a day where light would once again overtake the darkness.

As I was wheeled into that tunnel, I knew that moment had arrived. This transition to a highly qualified rehabilitation facility felt like my passport to recovery. I knew deep within that the staff here held strategies that could allow me to emerge not only out of the emotional dark, but also out of the heavy darkness that still held my body captive. My muscles had atrophied so much that lifting my arm to brush my fingers through my hair felt more like lifting a block of concrete. I had become so weak that my only hope was for God to guide me to a team of movement experts who would know how to take the broken pieces of my body and begin to strengthen them piece by piece until I could regain the simplest abilities that we all take for granted ... even as I was pushed through this tunnel toward that place, I began to dream, even if a bit cautiously, about what it would be like to walk from my car into work, to be able to shop for my own groceries, to have enough energy to walk on the beach with my mom and my friends. These simple joys had been taken for granted for over forty years … now they seemed like precious accomplishments that would allow me to transition from a world where sickness had become central to my daily life back to a place where relationships, joy and simple daily life would again become central.

The day had come. I was emerging out of the dark cocoon of transformation and I was about to learn how to fly … well, ok, I was about to learn how to walk. At this stage, walking would feel like it embodied the freedom and excitement of flying.

Just the move from hospital to rehabilitation marked an invitation to move from sickness to restoration, from sadness to hope, from stuck to freedom. I planned to get everything I could out of this experience.

I know my mom struggled, because once again she was not allowed to stay with me. Part of this "tunnel of change" was taking back the reins of my recovery and beginning to dare to do a few pieces of life on my own. While that was terrifying, it was also strangely liberating. I was going to miss my mom like a little girl misses home when she goes to camp for the first time. But we both knew this step contained keys to my emotional and mental recovery, just as it held hope for my physical recovery.

A long illness can often create a learned dependence on those around you as it erodes away at your confidence, your individuality and your freedom. *It had been my mom's season to exercise her ultimate strength … now it was my turn to do the same.* I knew this season would take all I had to give if I was going to succeed. The life-loving competitor deep within my soul kicked in. I had my game face on. I was ready for this challenge. Just like my Super Bowl playing champions, I was ready to emerge onto the field to give this game all I had to offer. I was more determined than ever to not let anything hinder me or slow me down. God had brought me this far. Now, I owed my best effort to Him and to those who had stayed by my side this entire time.

It was game day and I was determined to win. Like any championship game, I am now glad that I didn't know all of the hard hits that would come my way over the next few weeks. If I had known too much about what was on the other side of this tunnel, I would have grown discouraged right here in the tunnel. Today was simply a day to look forward and let the light that shone out of the darkness warm my weakened body and give hope to my weary heart. I was one step closer to going home!

Early in rehab, my mom received a call from one of my co-workers who had been through a similar illness. His advice was to take life one day at a time. He went on to tell her that today he is a runner. I cannot begin to explain what that did for my hope level. I even wondered if one day, I would be that "runner" bringing hope to others. In that moment, I realized that my hope was beginning to be restored. The evidence was in the fact that I was able to start looking beyond my bleak NOW further down the road to a beautiful FUTURE. Wow, that simple mental image felt like a beach breeze blowing through my hair.

Eleven people visiting were logged in mom's journal on

my first day in this new place. I had heard people going through illness and grief remark over the years that people are often forgotten after the first few days or weeks. We marveled that this was not our reality. Instead, the stream of family and friends who joined us in this fight felt more like a steady momentum building that kept gaining strength. I can assure each person who came that the momentum their love created carried me and my family through this dark time. Coupled with our deepening faith, people and God were our lifelines of hope. I cannot begin to express my gratitude for this army that surrounded me, fought for me and were positioned ready to celebrate with me.

Tuesday, April 29th was my first full day in rehab. I had a great nursing assistant who saw that my gown was clean and the fan was adjusted just right. I can almost read my mom's mind, as the great staff made it easier for her to rest when she could not be with me. I can feel the prayers on this first day as if they are lifting me higher.

I called Mom around lunch to proudly proclaim I had given myself a bath and dressed on my own ... well, there might have been some supervision. And my mom might have arranged my clothes in my closet neatly for each day. But this was a huge milestone. Day one was off to a great start! My parents both remarked that I was incredible ... they laughed at their assessment that I got only their good qualities and not the negative ones. They said they could see the best of both of them emerging to get me through this season. I just thanked God for making me in His image.

Another milestone was beginning to use a sliding board to bridge the distance from my wheelchair to any other surface, such as bed or an exercise mat. For all of this time, I had been lifted and moved by a mechanical lift that places you precariously in a sling, then hoists you into midair. For a person too weak to control their own body, this was a feeling that was frightening beyond words. I often felt as if I could slip out and fall to my death. Being assured by staff that I would not fall did little to alleviate the fears. Now, I was able to keep my own two feet on the ground while being transferred. I was literally and figuratively getting "grounded" back into daily life.

It grounded me further to begin to meet people whose diagnoses were more ominous than mine. I began to be even more aware of the value of this second chance I was receiving. My first roommate, Robin, was a young woman suffering from a brain tumor. She was a beautiful woman of faith and I knew we would inspire and encourage each other.

I could feel my confidence building toward the ultimate goal of walking out of here and being able to return to living independently. Some of those around me would never have that privilege. That saddened me and inspired me at the same time. It was almost as if I had an elevated sense of valuing each little gain I was making. I truly desired for all of the glory to go to the One who was bringing me through … Jesus Himself.

Prayer time with Mom had to be by phone tonight. I know the separation is as hard for her as it is for me. She said she missed holding my hand. I missed the comfort of her presence.

One benefit about Mom not being here is that I could

return to my morning call routine. Wednesday morning, I gave her a quick call in the midst of breakfast and getting ready for a busy day in therapy. *"Hey, Mom"* was a simple morning greeting we had enjoyed mindlessly. Now, each day that I was able to call and greet her from this place of growing health felt like a milestone in my recovery.

She says I asked her to bring shampoo and conditioner as I was preparing for my first real shower in months. Who would have ever thought that I would be celebrating sitting on a commode for the first time in over four months. Goodbye bed pans.

Again, eleven precious people stopped by to mark this day with me. Prayer time with Mom was full of thanksgiving and praise. Jesus is performing miracles and wonders. We both feel He has great things in store for my life. I grow hopeful and curious as to what the next season will hold.

The next few days, Mom and I really enjoyed starting our day with our phone call. I don't think I will take that simple pleasure for granted ever again. Faith really begins to take hold of my heart as I realize that God chose to spare me. I feel a fresh wave of blessing wash over me. I grow more determined than ever to honor God with all He has given back to me by doing my very best and giving the rest of my life to Him to use as He desires.

Mom told me that when she called to pay one of my bills, the woman who answered the phone already knew about my situation. Her church had been praying for me for weeks and she promised they would continue. I was amazed at how God is linking people together in this growing chain of blessing and victory. That one simple story caused me to marvel and to wonder just how many faithful people had joined in petitioning Heaven on my behalf.

I definitely needed those prayers of faith to continue for my full healing to become my reality. At this stage, limited endurance and poor vision were a couple of my biggest challenges. Early attempts to reduce the amount of oxygen I received failed. My body continued to require oxygen to be supplemented, as my weakened lungs were not strong enough to process enough air for my body. Even more of a practical concern was the damage to my eye sight from the stroke. I found it difficult to focus for tasks such as reading or using a calculator. My occupational therapist assessed this and created strategies to challenge and improve my vision. Mom reminded me of the survivor whose wisdom reminded me to simply take one day at a time.

GOD'S GOT THIS

Mom laughed as she recounted my early attempts at anything slightly independent, when I would say, *"I've got this."* This season of rehabilitation held physical, emotional and mental challenges that caused me to quickly revise that statement of self sufficiency to the right perspective of God sufficiency. I began to rightly proclaim, *"God's got this."*

Trying to regain the simplest of abilities works wonders to remind you that God is needed at every step along the way. When you are reduced to having someone else bathe you and brush your teeth, you gain a sense of smallness and weakness that can either launch you deep into despair or deep into faith. I chose faith! In a strange way, this season of weakness felt like it held the blessing of an awakened gratitude for all He permits me to do daily and all He does behind the scenes for me. I could really feel the hands of the Lord sustaining me, and I knew those hands had been there all along. I was just far less aware when my perception was one of self-sufficiency, not God-sufficiency.

In the first few days of rehab, Mom recorded in her journal that I called her to report my first normal blood tests since this whole ordeal began. These were the small victories that when strung together, would eventually lead me out of this place and back to my life.

My mom has always loved to celebrate and she declared now was the time to start planning our "Praise the Lord" party when I am discharged from the hospital. I wonder at this stage if she has any idea how her ongoing support and faith kept me holding onto hope? I could almost picture the party. Getting to see and hug the masses of friends and family who kept visiting the hospital even when they couldn't come into my room to actually see me. Seeing them and thanking them would be an overwhelming mile marker in this journey. I could hardly wait ... but I was still in the phase of taking one day at a time.

My mom was able to catch up on some work and life in these first few days when I was so busy with rehabilitating. She decided to stay home and talk with her own friends when she learned that my friends were planning to visit me here. I am so thankful for her presence and for her sensitivity to my need for rebuilding some independent connections of my own.

I stood up for 15 full minutes today. I know intuitively that walking is coming soon! I cannot explain what it feels like to know that day will come.

During our prayer time tonight by phone, my mom told me that she sees much evidence of my faith growing in this season. My heart is grateful that it shows and I see the same in her. It feels amazing to know this is strengthening us and drawing us closer, when you see so many tragedies dividing friends and families. My desire grows for this story to somehow be able to touch people who need their hope restored.

When Mom visited on Sunday, she insisted on washing my hair. This was supposed to be my day to rest and my body was screaming "No therapy, no activity." Mom logged in her journal that I was grumpy by the time we finished ... she also noted that I was losing my hair. The stress on my body was showing up even in my hair's inability to sustain itself. It had grown brittle, thin and fragile. This was another hurdle of humility and a place to sow into faith. As a hair dresser for nearly twenty years myself, the thought of losing my hair caused me to empathize with women being treated for cancer and other illnesses where a side-effect of treatment can be hair loss. While hair should feel like a minor issue, it was somehow connected to identity in a way that was difficult to express.

FIVE MINUTE PITY PARTY

Monday, May 6th, my faith wore thin. My shower came too early at 7:00 am and my tired body did not have time to prepare for the overwhelming task of bathing. I felt more like an invalid today than I had in days. My pressure sore was torn open during the transfer. I felt like crying but knew if I started, I might never stop. Mom told me it was OK to cry a few minutes, but then I had to return to my marvelous attitude. This honest and raw moment gave rise to our allowance of the "five minute pity party" where we would allow each other a short few moments of struggle as long as we agreed to return to that positive place of faith and hope.

That night, after Mom drove home, I called her to say goodnight. I thanked her for hanging in there with me. She later wrote in her journal that she was a lucky mom. She had then crossed out the word "lucky" and replaced it with the word "blessed." I knew in this season how important it was to credit God with all He was doing, and to not attribute any of it to luck. Fourteen precious people shared this day with me, cheering me on from the sidelines.

Tuesday, May 6th brought the best news I had since this ordeal began. I was given a tentative date to be discharged to home by the end of the month, give or take a few days.

Mom told me that she called Belaire to let them know how I was doing, as a few of the staff members had asked her to please keep them updated on my progress. Even though my time there wasn't all I had hoped it would be, I appreciated their ongoing concern and the contribution they made to my recovery.

This was also a day for us to attend a support and educational session for those affected by STROKE. That very word strikes terror in the hearts of those affected by it. While my vision and my left side gave me daily reminders that this had occurred, I was all too aware that the outcome could have paralyzed and disabled me for life. I was so grateful to have my parents there with me. My doctor also met with us and gave us encouraging news about his expectation for my recovery.

Eleven others visited and shared their hope today. Expectation and joy filled the air.

Our prayer time is growing in length, as mom now prays with me before she leaves for the night and again when we call to say goodnight.

Today, I called my mom so excited. The early morning baths and therapy had proven to be too much for my body but I couldn't seem to get the staff to understand. So, my doctor stepped in and blocked what he called "Sunrise days." In other words, it was now doctor's orders for me to be given time for my body to sleep in and rise at it was ready. This brought a huge wave of relief. I enjoyed knowing I could now schedule my own personal sunrise at any time I wished. I humorously mused that it would be great if I could get a life-long extension on this order. It might take me a lifetime of "sleeping in" to recover from this ordeal.

The days that followed were full of therapy and education that would prepare us for my discharge date. One thing that marked this season was how slowly I had to take everything. I know this was challenging for those around me, but trying to push at someone else's pace was just an impossibility that left me oxygen deprived and exhausted in bed. I found myself feeling tired often in this season and wondering if I would ever have enough energy to make it through a regular day.

Our prayer these days focused on asking God to strengthen my legs and to heal my vision. Therapy related to my eyes had revealed that both eyes were struggling, where it had been initially believed to be only my left eye caused by the stroke.

While I am anxious to walk, I am also encouraged that it is OK for that milestone to come last in my rehab stay. Insurance companies don't often look at the bigger picture of all patients need to regain, and I was told that if I walked too soon, insurance would demand a premature discharge from here, possibly causing me to miss out on critical therapy for other parts of my body. This allowed me to be at peace with my inability to walk. I knew it would come in time.

Thursday, May 8th, I called Mom before eight o'clock just like old times as I prepared to begin my day. My doctor stopped by and told me that my lungs are sounding clear and stronger. He also told me not to worry about the swelling in my feet and legs. He had faith that would resolve when I become more mobile. This all brought great encouragement for my day.

I was physically worn out after giving my all in therapy. One benefit is that the tiring days make for better sleep at night. In fact, I was already asleep today when my family came after therapy to visit.

My mom took time to coach me tonight, as I was growing anxious about having to take a shower tomorrow. Last time, my pressure sore had been re-opened and the early arising time had left my body exhausted and unable to co-operate. She encouraged me to talk with the therapist before the activities begin. I love how she is encouraging me to ex-ercise my voice, letting others know what I need. She also reminded me that fear is never from God.

This season of "firsts" required more faith, more pa-tience, more work and more endurance than I ever knew I possessed. In my weakest moments, oddly, I was finding out how strong I actually was. Staff, family and friends often commented on my attitude, faith and resolve. That made me more determined than ever to use this story to encourage others going through a hard or dark season of life.

On Friday morning, before that once-dreaded shower, Mom called to encourage me and to reinforce her coaching. My worries proved fruitless, not because the shower didn't go well. It didn't go at all. One of the hardest parts of this stage of my recovery is feeling totally at the mercy of every-thing changing at the last minute. I awoke with swollen feet, hands and a bladder infection. Coach Mom kicked in when she arrived, as I told her I felt this was a set-back. She refused to allow me to say those words. She reframed it as a small bump in the road.

My friend Robin played "How Great Thou Art" for me. This song had always been a favorite. Today, it was more than a favorite. It was a lifeline, linking my heart by faith to the hope of a future that was beginning to come into focus one day at a time. Dr. Tony Evans once said, *"Sometimes God lets you hit rock bottom so that you will discover that He is the Rock at the bottom."* Days like today held the power to do one of two things. I could plummet into hopelessness, or

I could rest my feet firmly on that Rock and shove myself back toward the surface, asking God to lift me high enough to view this from His perspective. Hopelessness or faith? I chose faith!

By Saturday, May 10th, I was feeling some better. Another antibiotic was now added to my overwhelming list of medications. My mom was faithful to remind me that our "Praise Party" was still going to happen as soon as I get home.

My bestie spent the day with me, providing the only medicine that I really needed to launch me free from the heaviness of the past few days. She gave me love and friendship. We had a great time together, talking, laughing and even going outside. Eleven other friends joined our celebration of friendship.

I continue to be amazed and encouraged by the lifeline of ongoing love, friendship and faith that presented itself over and over much like the safety net suspended under a high wire act. I knew on days when I felt like I had fallen, that the love and faith of others was there to catch me. My heart's desire grew to emerge out of this, not only healthy, but positioned to be that friend to others and to always speak life and faith. I like how V. Shavan states, *"Your success is directly proportional to the number of lives you have touched for the better."* Through all of this, I could almost feel my paradigm for life and success shifting. Priorities were being realigned. The value of life and love were being elevated. Vision for my future was being sculpted by the faith and by the pain. I had been given life once when I was born to my parents, once when Jesus saved me by faith (a salvation I continue to walk out daily), and now for a third time. This realization positioned my heart perfectly for the celebration to come tomorrow, Mother's Day.

Sunday arrived, May 11th. Mom wrote in her journal that it was her best Mother's Day ever. Her words echoed my heart: *"God, you chose to give Lauren life. How do I ever praise you enough?! Thank you, thank you, thank you."*

There it was ... she actually wrote "thank you" three separate times. It was almost as if she had read my mind from the day before. Thank you for the gift of being born to such amazing parents. Thank you for the gift of eternal salvation. Thank you for the hope of new life following this brush with death.

We spent the day reading, visiting, laughing. Ten others joined us.

The number ten is often considered to have spiritual significance of being the number that represents "testimony." I recalled John10:10. *"A thief comes only to steal and to kill and to destroy. I (Jesus) have come so that they may have life and have it in abundance."* This faith journey was teaching me how to discern God's voice and His hand. While many believe that sickness is given by God, I know it is only possible for God to give that which He possesses. Jesus is life, salvation, joy, peace and righteousness. It was the adversary of my life, satan himself, who had attacked me with the intent to steal, kill and destroy. But my Jesus was stronger and held the power and authority to redeem my life and give it back in abundance. I felt my own faith grow as my mom and I prayed daily to keep our hearts anchored firmly to the bedrock of His love and His ultimate plan.

The next week was filled with dealing with an ongoing bladder infection that robbed my limited endurance by making me feel sick and sluggish. I had to dig even deeper than usual to find the energy to push into my therapy sessions. Again, I was finding a reservoir of strength and determination that I never knew I possessed.

The greatest gift I received Monday, leading into Tuesday, was the gift of sleeping all night. It amazed me how much difference resting well made in my overall endurance level.

Therapy included working on the standing machine and the parallel bars, and spending time on the seated elliptical machine. I had a shower that was not a total disaster. I was able to wash my own hair. Fourteen people stopped by on a Tuesday to encourage my journey. This ongoing support never ceases to amaze and delight me!

MY FIRST FOUR STEPS

Wednesday, May 14th, was a banner day ... I took four steps in therapy! Whoever thought taking four steps could feel as gratifying as walking four miles? Well, it did. While I felt just as tired, I also felt just as accomplished. I called my mom just as she was pulling into the post office parking lot. She said it made her feel like getting out on the sidewalk and shouting, *"My daughter walked today."* I would love to have been there to see if she actually did this or not.

My therapist further encouraged me that I was making great progress and was on track with my therapy goals. I rested in bed with an awesome sense of accomplishment and a cold drink. You might have to be Southern like me to understand how important it was for this milestone to be celebrated with diet Mountain Dew. I called my work family at MDI with my latest news.

Later in the day, Mom and Dad visited together. We had a great time laughing and celebrating. I later shared with them how much it blessed me for them to come together as they had on my behalf, even sharing tender moments praying and listening to God. I had heard stories of them doing this when I was a little girl, but I didn't remember those early years. Today's time together, I was sure I would never forget.

Thursday, May 5th, I awoke to a weather alert on my phone regarding a tornado warning for the Charlotte area. This was my new neighborhood while here in rehab. While it wasn't the best way to start my day, I figured I had already survived worse. The winds of change had already demolished much of what I had once taken for granted. The storm passed with no major damage despite the impending threats. I took that as a prophetic sign that I would one day emerge out of this storm with no major damage, and with some great stories of faith to share.

I graduated from speech therapy today, as my swallowing ability returned to normal. This leaves more time to concentrate on getting my body ready to get out of here. Mom shared my excitement and marked the day by setting an official date for our "Praise the Lord" party. In faith, we set July 12th aside as our day to celebrate all God has done and to create a deserved place where all of our friends and family could come together to be celebrated for their place in my recovery. Because my life was now a miracle, many had sown into this miracle and deserved to receive part of the blessing.

Today, eighteen people visited and I took seventeen steps. My therapist said tomorrow I could graduate out of the parallel bars onto a walker. I feel freedom begin to beckon to me from outside these walls. My discharge cannot come soon enough, but I need to stay focused so I get the maximum benefit from these days in therapy.

While there were plenty of moments to celebrate, I also continued to lose more hair ... there seemed to always be some sobering reminder of the magnitude of the storm I just came through. Instead of discouraging me, I chose to let these challenges remind me of how far I had come, fueling my faith that I would recover completely. Maybe one day, I would find myself in the news as the girl who faced a storm but came out with no major damage. The winds of devastation were losing their grip and the winds of hope, faith and future were taking over.

Saturdays used to mean the weekend. Now, it meant getting up early on someone else's schedule for therapy. I did ten grueling minutes on the elliptical to warm up for more walking and practicing transfers. Fourteen people gave up part of their weekend to come by and smile on my progress.

Sunday, I was ready to rest. A nursing assistant accidentally brushed my foot while moving a pillow, setting off pain caused by neuropathy, damage to my nerve endings. The pain lingered, again reminding me that my body has a long way to go. Mom logged ten sweet visitors today.

My phone charger died Monday, maybe as a sign that I need to rest more and talk less. My body is still showing signs of struggle, as my feet and face are red and splotchy with a rash that feels tight and burns. My mom prayed again for God's healing to wash over me from the top of my head to the soles of my feet. He is my only hope! He is my Great Physician! My parents are His blessing to my journey, constantly reminding me to keep my eyes on what He is doing even when the details of the day try to distract or discourage me.

Tuesday, May 20th, the doctor told me that he could actually hear air beginning to move in my lungs, evidence the ARDS is beginning to heal. While I still need oxygen constantly, the amount I am receiving is reduced again.

Mom prayed again that beautiful head-to-toe healing prayer, as the cream they tried on my face made it worse and my bladder infection continues to hold on.

My discharge date was delayed today by a full week, and I broke down and cried. The new date is set for June 3rd, 2014. My mom had actually encouraged the doctor to keep me longer so I could be more ready. I know she is right for the sake of my safety, but I had to throw my emotions into reverse and try to pull myself mentally back into this place when I had begun to taste freedom beyond these walls. I have been in the hospital over four months. Right now, a one-week delay felt like another year's prison sentence.

The Lord gave me grace and I found myself feeling more hopeful as I awoke on Wednesday. I made the decision to stop drinking diet Mountain Dew in case this might be irritating my bladder or feeding the infection. I continue to increase the distances I walk with the walker in therapy. The wheelchair is still required as my walking is labored and requires assistance for safety. When Mom arrived, my roommate and I were up in our chairs hanging out for dinner time. The three of us talked and laughed.

IDENTITY SHIFT

My mom and I discussed the news of two individuals who had similar illnesses but did not survive. We both marvel at the gift of life that has been given to me. I have survived. Now my prayers shifted to, *"Lord, show me why I have survived. I don't want to miss Your Divine Purpose."*

A friend would remark to me months down the road a revelation that gave a glimpse into my ultimate life purpose. This friend drove by my former place of employment, MDI which stands for Merchants Distributors Incorporated. When my friend saw the MDI sign, the Lord spoke to her and prompted her to call me with the new meaning embedded in those three simple letters. They now stood for Mastering Divine Identity. My identity was certainly being reshaped through this journey into one that found less significance in the externals of work, body image, the opinions of others, and the status of cars and clothes.

I was being awakened to value the abilities we take for granted daily such as walking, breathing and caring for ourselves. My new identity was shifting my value off of the externals of where you work and how good your hair looks to the fact that I lived another day and hold the power to encourage others. I now looked at every step and every breath as a personalized gift right from the hand of God. The pull of the world system was weakening as my heart became more and more determined to live a life that would allow my story to bring others into alignment with their divine identity in Christ Jesus. Perhaps, as I master my own divine identity, I would be given the honor to bless others with some of the life lessons and faith that emerged out of this storm.

The therapy staff gave Mom instructions on how to measure the doorways in her home to make sure my custom wheelchair would fit. I would also need my own walker and a brace to support the weakness in my left leg caused by the stroke months earlier. All of this adaptive equipment was making me feel a bit high maintenance. A family therapy day was scheduled so that my family could work with me and the therapy staff for several hours to prepare for the shift in my care out of the hands of the rehab staff into the hands of my family. I thank God again and again for such faithful parents and a safe place to return. Bubble gum was the simple pleasure of my day. Had anyone ever been truly grateful for bubble gum other than me? It felt like a reason to celebrate just having enough energy to chew, the ability to swallow and the air capacity to blow a few obnoxious bubbles.

Mom and I included my roommate in our prayer time tonight. I quietly ask God to watch over her after I leave. I will miss her. I want her to have the same joy of healing and freedom that I am experiencing.

On Friday, May 23rd, I battled discouragement again over my extended stay. The staff and Mom explained to me that I needed several hours of therapy a day and would need a nurse upon my discharge home. They feared that home health would not be intense enough to keep me progressing consistently, and they reminded me that I could not have a home health nurse if I chose outpatient therapy over home health. The bureaucracy of the insurance system and the financial side of illness was a battle in and of itself. I was so thankful to my Mom for carrying this burden for me, yet my heart ached at the weight and stress this has placed on her in a time when she had to be so present for me. Fourteen precious visitors lifted my heavy heart back toward Heaven.

I found myself in one moment, frustrated that I would have to return to living with my Mom, only in the next moment to find myself fearing being alone. What if something were to happen to her? Oh, Lord, please protect her. I knew she was my only link to life beyond these walls. That thought brought a simultaneous barrage of emotions which spanned from gratitude to fear. I was profoundly aware that this war would not end the moment I am finally discharged. That would just be the first day of the newest battle in this war to regain my health and my freedom … the transition "home."

We included Robin again tonight in our prayer time. She and I both realize that we may have to accept some unwanted changes along the way. Mom prays and encourages us both. I'm so blessed that she is my mom!

The weekend brought much-needed rest and a number of visitors, ten on Saturday and twelve on Sunday. While there might be some doubts about the future, I could never doubt that I am loved and valued. I began to mentally prepare myself for my final week of rehab. I knew they would all push me to excel, in preparation to be discharged home.

Monday, May 26th marked Memorial Day and my final Monday of inpatient rehabilitation. I think of my grandfather and the medals he brought home from World War II. Many families would ponder those who had been lost in the effort to maintain our freedom in this nation. I am thankful that a day of Memorial can be a celebration for my family, as the somber nature of this holiday reminds me of how close I came to being a casualty of this war that assaulted my body way back in January. Months have passed and I bear a few battle scars, but I am alive to wave the flag of freedom and honor those who were taken prematurely. We enjoyed our own Memorial Day Celebration over a meal outside, the closest we could come to a real cookout.

Last week, the thought of an extra week depressed me. This week, I found myself begging the doctor for another extension in my stay as I realized how far I still have to go. Mom and I were overwhelmed with details of my complex daily routine of medicines, along with the fears of how I will adapt to her home out of this controlled environment. I had learned to transfer from my wheelchair to my walker, from my bed to the chair. But everything would be different at home. Different chairs. Narrow doorways. The safety of rehab was about to give way to that of a return to real life in an unpredictable setting.

Tuesday I learned that my request for one extra week of inpatient therapy had been granted. I really felt that this would allow me to gain more strength and more confidence before my discharge. It also gave me peace to know this would reduce Mom's stress about the upcoming transition that would alter both of our lives. We were both used to living alone, so our independence and routine were about to be put to the test.

The decision was made that I would follow up with home health therapy instead of outpatient therapy, as the staff felt strongly that the fragile nature of my medical status warranted the need for a nurse to visit regularly during my transition back home.

Today's therapy focused on walking and on dressing independently. I am reminded again of my dependence as we discuss what type of bed I will need at home, along with other details on adaptations that will be required for my new way of life as a person with a temporary disability. I have faith that this is only temporary.

My friend knew just what I needed today. She brought a beautiful card which included the poem, "Footprints in the Sand." (Author Unknown) While I always thought it was inspirational, it never held quite as much significance in my walking days as it did now. The poem illustrates a person wondering where God was when he could only find one set of footprints, only to find that the footprints belonged to God as the person was being carried. As able-bodied people going through life unaware of the magnitude of our daily blessings, we are lulled into a false belief that we are self sufficient. In reality, we are being carried along every day by the God who created us. The poem took on new meaning now that I was unable to walk without help, and could easily recognize the one set of footprints as those belonging to Jesus who had carried me through this ordeal. I stopped right in that moment, and ask God to keep this revelation fresh in my heart, especially as I regain strength. While I do want to be independent, I never want to return to a sense of independence so great that it causes me to forget or to ignore my need for God to journey with me. I pray this one simple truth will always be part of my story from this day forward.

Wednesday, May 28th, I got off to a slow start with my day not beginning until 11:00 am. I hate to admit it, but I love a slow start to my morning. This is certainly a rare pleasure that I always took for granted.

Therapy was good today and I had an overwhelming sense that God was carrying me again. Seventeen people shared the day by visiting and a ramp building project got underway at Mom's house for my wheelchair. Mom has always been a bit of a neat-nick so I am burdened for how all of the changes to her home might cause her stress. It is hard enough knowing I cannot return to my own home, only to have that compounded by feeling like I am disrupting someone else's world. *"God, give me peace and joy in this season as you bring unity to Mom and me."*

I got discouraged as symptoms suggested another bladder infection. At this point, anything that could affect my discharge date felt like a major hurdle and I found myself quickly moving from a place of faith to fear. A few staff members got frustrated over my need to have assistance getting out of bed multiple times to go to the bathroom. Their frustration only reinforced my dependence and made me feel like an invalid. That is a funny word, even as I write it. Invalid can be broken down into two words, in and valid. It saddens me to realize that our culture has chosen to use language that devalues as in-valid individuals who do not function "normally." While many people live well and accomplish great things from the reality of life with a disability, society handicaps people with labels that rob them of their God-given value and dignity.

I sense that this concept will emerge as one of the parts of my story, as I find myself struggling to recognize my own value now that I require daily assistance from professionals and family. While the world would say I am now worth less since I cannot walk far, work or fully care for myself, God shouts out that our value is found within the heart. We have value because He has given us life and because He calls us sons and daughters. Jesus died on the cross after simply stating, *"It is finished."* Part of what was finished in that moment was the battle over our significance. While the enemy will never give up on trying to de-rail our identity, one simple truth remains … I have value that is incomparable simply because God created me and sustains me into eternity. I have nothing left to prove or to gain that could ever cause Him to love me or to value me more. I find great comfort on this hard day as His truth settles deep into my heart.

INFLUENCE DENIED

Pastor Bill Johnson once said, *"Faith doesn't deny a problems existence. It denies it a place of influence."* I knew that my emotional, mental and spiritual recovery would be every bit as important as my physical recovery. This would begin by me refusing to give my current limitations any power to depress or oppress me.

My co-author shared this concept with me. God created with the spoken word. We see evidence of this in the Genesis

Biblical account of creation. God goes on to tell us that we were created in His image. So, here is the powerful revelation. If God created by speaking and we are made like Him, we create by speaking. I had to stop and ask if I was creating life or death through my thoughts and words. What are you speaking over your own life, your family and your current set of circumstances? Speak life and choose joy.

Another author also says it well. *"Happiness is an inside job. Don't assign anyone else that much power over your life."* Mandy Hale It occurred to me that it would be a terrible insult to the God who had saved me from death to allow the enemy of my soul any voice in this situation. Whether the enemy tries to talk to you himself, through the brokenness of others or through your own negative thoughts, displace his voice with the Voice of your Creator, Jesus. Speak scripture over yourself. Repeat positive, life-giving affirmations from family and friends. Transform the words you speak over yourself from negative to positive. For example, we need to stop saying we want to die for things, such as *"I would die for a piece of chocolate."* We need to speak life. We need to choose life! We owe it to our Creator, ourselves and those within the realm of our influence. It is simple ... I have come this far only because God used those around me to speak life and hold onto faith.

God has brought me this far. I cannot give in to fear, doubt or negativity now. The game is still underway and the final score has not been recorded. I want the testimony of a land-slide victory. I don't want to barely make it through this. I want my life to astonish onlookers. If my life is going to point others to the Light of God's unfailing love and healing power, I have to keep choosing His perspectives over the darkness of my circumstances.

This attitude is not coming from being in a place where this now comes easy. I had to choose this attitude in the heat of the battle. Even at this stage, finding it impossible to summon the strength to roll over in bed without help, I have been forced flat onto my back for nearly five months. Well, if the number five Biblically represents God's grace, I need an extra measure of that grace to get through these final few days of rehab and transition home safely into my new life.

Friday, May 30th, brings news that the ramp building project is still underway. Several men volunteered to do this for us. I am reminded that Jesus was a carpenter. These men feel like extensions of His hands and craftsmanship skills today as they lay down a path that will give me access to my new life and home.

I felt good today and full of hope. Mom relayed the most beautiful story of a lady stopping her today outside of the library in her home town to pray for us. I enjoyed time with some of my girl friends. Simone de Beauvoir once said, *"That's what I consider true generosity. You give your all, and yet you feel as if it costs you nothing."* My friends and family seemed to have a supernatural grace and endurance. They gave and gave, never once seeming inconvenienced or burdened. I wonder if I will ever truly be able to convey to them how their generosity and love were the forces that rehabilitated my heart, while the therapists rehabilitated my body.

Saturday, Mom and I both mused over the first-class care I had received here. We were both incredibly grateful for the progress I had made and for the investment of education and equipment that would make going home possible. I had once feared having to be released from rehab to a skilled nursing facility, a real threat if I had not gained the strength sufficient to walk and participate in my own care. I now knew I was headed home and that thought alone caused the wind to fill the sails of my heart. I almost felt as powerful as the mighty sail boats I had admired on past trips to the coast. I had been anchored to hospitals since January, and was ready for the open water of life after rehab. The adventures ahead began to tug on my heart, and I emotionally began to release myself into this next phase of my recovery … home on my own terms. Thirteen people shared their Saturday selflessly with us. How would I ever repay the love and support?

Sunday I awoke surprised to receive exactly what I ordered for breakfast, a bacon, egg, cheese sandwich. I wonder how well Mom will adapt to my new expectation of breakfast in bed at home? We laugh at the thought. In reality, I should be the one serving her for the next few months, but that will have to wait just a while until I am strong enough to navigate the kitchen on my own.

While several visitors also came by on Sunday, all I could think of was going out to visit someone else. I couldn't wait to be able to stop by a friend's home, go out to dinner or just hang out at a family member's home on the weekend.

Mom and I got a good laugh out of my account on Monday of getting to practice transferring to and from a car, using an old rusted out Buick they kept in the parking lot for this purpose. I quipped that it was "hell-la-ish." Looking back, I would have gladly taken the out-of-date car for a spin if it cranked and I had the strength to drive. "Hell-la-ish" or not, it would not have been safe to put motorized wheels under me and have them this close to the open highway. Everything in me wanted to hop behind the wheel and just keep driving. It felt good just being outside and knowing that I was now one therapy goal closer to actually hitting the open road for home.

I had fun practicing the sign language I had learned way back in Girl Scouts to "talk with" a girl who was hearing impaired that attended a group session I was part of today.

Mom's highlight of the day was telling me about how well plans are coming on our party and how much she is appreciating the input and hard work of dear friends.

It was Tuesday, June 3rd, as details continued to fall into place. My need for supplemental oxygen continued to be reduced, my blood thinner shots were stopped, and my endurance for being up out of bed continued to increase.

Thursday, June 5th, was set aside as another family education day. We feel more prepared this time around. I know Mom is anxious about caring for me on her own. These past two weeks of therapy were the windfall I needed to get stronger and to build confidence. You know you are doing well when your therapist sets new goals after you surpass your original goals.

The weekend brought more waves of nervous excitement about going home next week, mingled with the sober awareness of how different life is going to be now. These stressful thoughts are compounded by physical signs that my body is struggling to adapt to the increased activity, with my feet and legs swelling and hurting more. I can't help but wonder how I will stay calm – and keep Mom calm – when I can no longer call for the nurse to ask a question or have a medical need quickly assessed.

I love this quote by Jim Elliott: *"The sound of 'gentle stillness' after all the thunder and wind have passed will be the ultimate Word from God."* My faith is all I have to stand on as I head home. This storm certainly came with several rounds of loud thunder and raging winds of change. On one hand, I pray for all to be calm as I go home, with no complications, no falls, no new crisis. On the other hand, I feel an ominous sense of how quiet an empty house is going to be for hours and days on end. I have survived the noise of the storm. Now I have to survive the quiet of a life that has temporarily come to a screeching halt. I am being told that visitors should be limited due to my weakened immune system and that I should limit my own activity.

This onslaught of thoughts reminds me of one other favorite verse: *"Be still, and know that I am God!"* Psalm 46:10a (NLT) Upon quick inspection, this verse sounds as if it is telling us to be still in order to come to know God on a higher level. That actually isn't correct. When you study the original word that was translated "be still," it really means to be in shock and awe as to who God is and all He is capable of … *so shocked that it leaves a person frozen, unable to move.*

I know I am coming into a season of forced stillness as my body continues to recover. While my body may be in a state of limited activity, I can choose to still my spirit to receive a revelation of all God has done to sustain me. I am living a reality that is now made up of a collective series of miracles. I find myself asking God to bring a continual awareness of all Jesus has done to make my return home possible, while also bringing daily gratitude, awe and awareness of how He is sustaining me and my family.

If I have just endured the season of RECOVERY, my highest hope is to enter my season of RESTORATION. The Merriam Webster dictionary defines restoration as: to give back someone or something that was lost or taken, to bring back into existence or use, to return to an earlier condition by repairing it.

Monday, June 9th, 2014, marks the ultimate milestone to date in this adventure. It marks my final day in therapy, almost five full months since this ordeal began. My mood was light as I finished therapy by noon while my father picked up and delivered all of my adaptive equipment that would be required for daily life at home. Home health is scheduled to come and assess me once I'm released. While final details fall into place, I stop counting days and begin counting HOURS!

The most overwhelming thought is that of every "first" ... my first attempt at doing life without the supervision and assistance of trained professionals, my first time getting up the ramp into the house, my first time getting into a bed that doesn't adjust easily, the first time getting into a bathroom that is not fully accessible.

While I know I will be anxious, my heart also goes out to my mom. I know she is about to receive an honorary doctors degree, nurses degree and therapy degree as the weight of the responsibility will now fall on her. This could lead to a new nick-name, Dr. Mom. She may like this title better than Mama lion.

Even though I will soon be home, thirteen faithful friends visit on this final day as a reminder that I was never forgotten this entire time. I have watched many patients with few to no guests and wonder how anyone gets out of a situation like this alive without the advocacy and love of a great support system. I pray over those I will be leaving behind to feel supported and loved. I feel a wave of hope wash over me that I am indeed transitioning from recovery to restoration. *This new season cannot begin soon enough.*

In the months just prior to my illness,
living my day to day life, I could never have imagined
the challenges that lay ahead of me. Now on this side
of my mirculous journey, I would challenge everyone
to never take a single breath for granted.

Me and my daddy, Lum Summey.

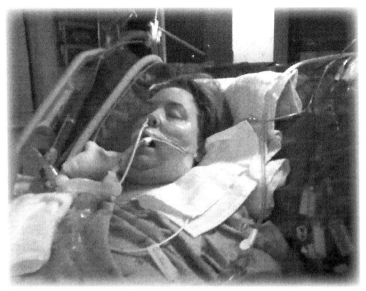

As 2014 began, I spent 6 weeks in a coma fighting for my life.

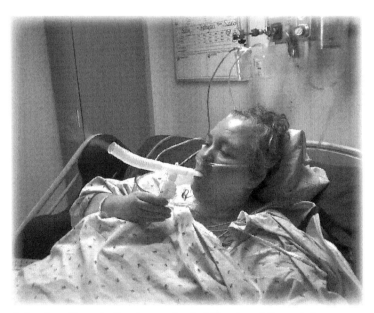

Months of hospitalization and rehabilitation followed the coma.
This was the hardest work I had ever done.

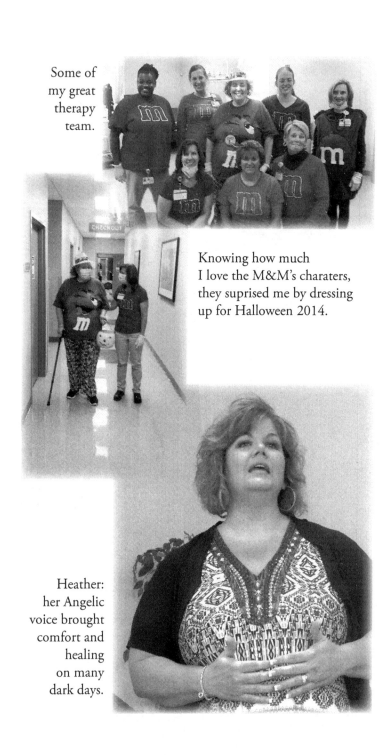

Some of my great therapy team.

Knowing how much I love the M&M's charaters, they suprised me by dressing up for Halloween 2014.

Heather: her Angelic voice brought comfort and healing on many dark days.

"Praise the Lord Party" July 2014.

Me and my girls.

Me celebrating new life with Mom and Dad.

Me and Mom at Myrtle Beach, June 2015. Dreaming of the
beach brought hope and motivation on my hardest days.

Me singing, "How Great Thou Art"
to thank the One who brought me this far.

Chilling at the beach and dreaming of the future.

Dressed up for my 45th birthday party. More grateful than ever!

BEYOND RECOVERY TO RESTORATION

CHAPTER 7

*"Accept what is. Let go of what was.
And have faith in what will be."*
—*Zig Ziglar*

This day finally arrived! June 10th, 2014. I am going home. The discharge process was complicated and lengthy, with follow-up appointments, discharge instructions and multiple prescriptions needing to be filled by the hospital pharmacy. A couple of friends visited, providing a needed distraction and stress relief. Sarah made plans to spend the night with Mom and me. I know that will ease the transition.

The plan was for Mom to work while Wayne and Dad, both retired, would rotate shifts. Wayne would come in the morning and cook breakfast, alternating in the afternoon with Dad so he could help with my home therapy.

Wednesday, June 11th was my first full day home. Home health arrived with a nurse and an occupational therapist (the professional skilled to assist a person in re-learning personal care skills). They approved me for a nursing aide who will assist me with my personal hygiene until I am able to fully care for myself. Mom works to get my medicines organized, not a simple job with a box full of bottles larger than the tool box that a carpenter would carry. It was also the beginning of my wearing a face mask when I am around anyone.

I feel the overwhelming love and support of my parents and friends who are committed to seeing me through this journey. At the same time, I feel the weight of the road ahead of me. My life is now reduced from productive and fun to learning how to get into a regular bed so I can get rid of this hospital bed that was loaned to us. My special-order wheelchair doesn't fit through the doors, so I opt to use my grandfather's wheelchair and quickly find it comforting, almost as if his arms are around me. My mom, a person who values order, is having her exceptionally neat environment cluttered with oxygen cords, doors taken off the hinges, boxes, and more medicine than spices on her kitchen counter. The visual reminder of how much I am changing her world is an emotional reminder of how much my life feels in disarray. She assured me it was just stuff and that the only thing that mattered to her was that I am still alive.

Graham Cooke once said, *"When we have an outlook that is focused on the past, we are cultivating a life incompatible with God's perception."* I knew that I was going to have a find a new way to view this season in order to not fall into bondage to despair over all that had been lost. I had to hold onto faith and ask God to reveal His perspectives on this new season so I could see it through His eyes, not through my own thoughts and emotions.

I am finding out that when we position ourselves to see our lives from His higher vantage point, we have already moved into victory. A new perspective has the power to shift an ongoing set of circumstances to a whole new level. The same things can take on a whole new meaning. The doors coming off the hinges began to remind me that God is opening new doors for me. The oxygen cord that created my short leash in life could also remind me that without God breathing new life into me, I would not be here to experience this transition. I was reminded of His breath of life every time I rolled over that cord, wheeling from one room to the next. I was being given new eyes to see the past five months through His lenses, and I had hope that a new life could emerge out of the darkest place.

Thursday, after only two days home, I had to make an appointment to visit Dr. Habashi who was now going to be my primary care physician. I put on my leg brace for the first time, hoping to be able to walk more and gain strength.

Mom and I continue our prayer times, with today's prayers focusing on our overwhelming gratitude for how far I have come. We also discuss our "praise the Lord party" that is scheduled for one month away, right around my birthday. It feels amazing to have so much to celebrate. We choose to focus on what we have to celebrate instead of all that is lost.

Friday the 13th held no negative superstition for me. I was told I should be walking and not using the chair much within three months. Therapy is going well. My home health nurse is an encourager.

Saturday brought a quiet day of rest. Dad visited and

helped out in the afternoon, bringing a flashlight in case the power ever goes out, as I cannot burn candles due to my oxygen dependency. The little details can often feel like overwhelming reminders of how fragile my health still is.

God wanted me to recall how powerful He still is and He used a friend to remind me. A precious Godly mentor and her husband visited, praying over me and anointing me with oil. The peace and refreshing I felt as she prayed was nothing short of supernatural. Sixteen other people came by. The love is still overwhelming and the waves keep coming.

I find myself dreading nights, as the darkness reminds me of the coma. I know Mom feels my anxiety as her night time prayers often focus on asking God to allow me to rest well. This particular night I did rest well, awakening on Sunday feeling rested and ready for a pedicure. Blue was my new color. I read a few of my many cards as my new polish dried. I had my hair washed with real shampoo, not that institutional junk that leaves you smelling like a medicine cabinet. I found it easier to get into and out of the bathroom, evidence I am still gaining strength. I enjoyed a few visits from friends in the afternoon and was weary by the evening.

DOCTORS DO CRY

Monday, June 16th was another amazing day. Today, I finally met the doctor who helped save my life, Dr. Neveen Habashi. I was in a coma when she had come to the first hospital while others doctors were away attending a conference. Mom and I learned today that she was not even supposed to be in town that particular day. She had just returned exhausted from another conference. She was busy catching up on her own work; therefore, she had originally turned down the request. She said, that while she did not feel she had the time because of being busy with her own practice, she kept having a "feeling" that she should be there. She finally called them back and agreed to come. The simple fact that she followed her instincts quite possibly saved my life. Remember, she was also the one whose brother was a physician doing critical research in ARDS, the life-threatening problem that attacked my lungs. In other words, she turned out to be a double blessing.

When Dr. Habashi walked into the room, she immediately began to cry. She quickly stated, *"Your prognosis was so grim that no one thought you were going to survive."* We all had a good laugh as she composed herself. Her compassion poured over us like healing oil. She told Mom right there that she had single handedly *"willed me to live"* by being so present and by determining to speak life over me constantly in those early weeks. She also reminded Mom that she had done the right thing all the times she felt she needed to push in order to get the care I needed. It was reassuring to have an actual physician tell Mom that she was right and not out of order. She even went on to say how much each patient needs a strong advocate watching out for them in love because it is not a perfect system.

Dr. Habashi gave me encouragement during this visit, being most sensitive to the fragile stage of my emotional recovery. Behind the scenes, she felt prompted once again. This time she followed that lead to take time to craft a medical summary of the critical nature of my illness. She entrusted the following summary to me and Mom at a later time, giving us full permission to review it and share it as we felt led. While my Mom had written from a personal perspective, it felt invaluable to have this dear physician take time to journal from the other side of my hospital bed, as she cared for me when my life was held in the balance between life and death. It is included here just as she created it to honor her efforts and to give you a glimpse into the miraculous medical team and countless healings that God orchestrated on my behalf. Here is the letter she shared with us:

Hi Lauren and Susan,

Your book is going to be amazing and inspiring. I couldn't put it down. A few things I want to point out, please use at your discretion.

1. When they called me to ask me to moonlight, I said no because I was very busy that week in the office and could not find coverage. I asked them to find someone else and to call me only if they couldn't find anyone. I felt sure they could find someone because there is a pool of intensivists that they could call. They could not find anyone and kept calling me, and I kept saying I couldn't. One of the lead physicians called me personally and said they really needed me otherwise he could not go to the conference. I kept thinking there must be a reason they keep calling and I kept asking myself why do I have this compulsion that I have to go and help out even though I knew it was nearly impossible because I had a full schedule and no coverage. So I said alright and somehow, by the grace of God, I was able to arrange coverage at the last minute and reschedule the patients.

2. *When I saw Lauren, she was on maximal ventilator support, using conventional ventilation. The pressures required from the ventilator were extremely high. That's why she had that air under her skin because her lungs were about to rupture. Despite this high pressure we were unable to adequately oxygenate her. Additionally with this much pressure from the ventilator, it is nearly impossible to allow the patient to wake up from sedation and stop the paralytics because that much pressure in the lung is difficult for patients to tolerate. They cannot breathe with the ventilator without being medically paralyzed.*

3. *My brother, Dr. Nader Habashi, is a professor at the University of Maryland and is a leading authority on APRV, a new mode of ventilation that does not rupture the lungs, is more physiologically sound and less traumatic to the lung, and is a much more comfortable mode of ventilation as it allows the patient to tolerate the ventilator without paralytics. Using this mode of ventilation, he has saved thousands of lives with some of the most severe cases of ARDS. He has written countless articles, book chapters and is continuing his ongoing research to prove to the medical community that this is the best way to oxygenate ARDS patients.*

4. *The medical community is not readily accepting of this mode. Why? Because it is labor intensive, requires a working knowledge of the ventilator and lung mechanics, and flies in the face of conventional wisdom. My brother has lectured in the United States and in countries all over the world. He is very humble and does not do this for fame or recognition but because he is convinced that this mode of ventilation has saved and can save many more lives.*

5. *I believe that it was the BIVENT mode, the APRV analogue on the particular machine that Lauren was on which saved her life. This mode allowed her lungs to heal, and allowed her to recruit lung units that were not participating in air exchange. Without this mode, we would have not been able to discontinue the paralytics and allow her to wake up.*

6. *In that week that she was on BIVENT/APRV we saw tremendous improvement in her lung mechanics, and luckily the physician who resumed her care when he returned from the conference continued that for a few more days after I left, and was gracious enough to confer with my brother which gave enough time for her lungs to be salvaged, even though it was late in the game. I hope and pray that your book, among all of the great things that I know it will do, will bring attention to this mode of ventilation which can greatly impact the treatment of ARDS and save many lives.*

7. *There were times, more than I care to remember, when we almost lost Lauren. Each time I was busy with other patients but I had this indescribable force drawing me back upstairs to her room. It was always when she was on the verge of catastrophe. I cannot explain it. One day the air from under her skin had organized into her lung and it could have collapsed her lung and killed her instantly. Luckily I was able to get the cardiothoracic surgeon to come put a tube in her chest, and avoid this potential disaster. I stood in the room with him the entire time and prayed knowing that inserting the tube in itself could lead to another disaster and I had to be there just in case. God was with us and the procedure went smoothly.*

8. *The General surgeon felt reluctant to put in the tracheostomy because it was very risky and she could die from the*

procedure. I told him not to worry about it and I left instructions with the staff nurse to consult with the ENT physicians for the tracheostomy and to please make sure that the ENT did the tracheostomy the following week, since we were able to reduce the pressures on the ventilator and it would be safer then. In my training, ENT were the ones most comfortable with that procedure in high risk patients, and sure enough when I checked in with the nurses the following week, they were amazed as were the Doctors at how smoothly the procedure went.

9. My week there affirmed my faith in God, working through medical professionals that He lined up in the sequence He wanted to save Lauren so that she could inspire the entire world with her story of courage and hope.

10. I am certain that your book will be a tremendous success and a blessing to the world. You are right. God was there the whole time.

On the day of my first visit to her office, we left with a fresh reminder of how God's hand had directed and orchestrated countless details, some we could see and many we may never be aware of, all contributing to the gift of life I am enjoying today. As I re-read Dr. Habashi's medical summary, I am reminded in a fresh way just how blessed I am to be alive with a story to share.

I now choose to focus on all I have been given, not what is lost. I find myself awakening to God's new purpose for this new life I have been given. One simple thing would make this all worth enduring ... *for one person to find hope in their own situation.*

Heidi Baker, an awe-inspiring missionary to Mozambique says it this way: *"Don't waste your time consumed with what makes you weak. Spend your time pressing in for the Presence. Become so intimate with Jesus, so full of Him, that it does not matter what challenges in life present themselves to you. You will be so spiritually full that you can feed a multitude of other people's needs. Jesus will give you more than enough."*

Could it be possible that God would prompt me, much as He had prompted Dr. Habashi, to now come alongside others as a life line? Could it be possible that I had been allowed to experience all of this in order to share the lessons learned through a God-centered lens? Could it be possible that someone would choose to live in hope instead of fear because of this journey I had endured? That would truly make it all worthwhile.

Over the next few days, I enjoyed good therapy sessions, special ordered a few of my favorite foods and enjoyed the quiet of home and my Mother's love. My feet and legs continued to hurt, providing a reminder that my body is still healing. I like what Bill Johnson has to say: *"Don't let the absence of an immediate breakthrough change your revelation of God's nature."* These days were going to feel slow and labored, but they were not the sign that I had been forgotten or left behind by the Healing God. My days were now a slow, ongoing reminder that Jesus had kept me alive for a purpose that has not been fully revealed.

On Thursday, June 19th, now just over five months since this all began, I called Mom into the room. Instead of asking for a snack or my next medicine, I asked her to stand in front of my wheelchair. I slowly stood up, steadied myself, let go of the chair and wrapped her in a hug of gratitude. She emotionally called this her *"Mother's Moment"* as this was the first "real" hug I had given her since January 12th. I find that I am gaining confidence in walking and in living. I am alive and I know it is for a purpose that will be revealed. I cannot wait to understand more of my new assignment for this next season of life.

Mom told me that the next day, when she left for work, she first took time to stand and watch me sleep and breath on my own. The only thing needed was a bit of supplemental oxygen. She said this spontaneous prayer, *"Thank you, Lord. What a beautiful sight to watch my daughter lay there and breathe. I stand in awe of your miracles. Thank you, Lord. Her 'Praise the Lord' party is getting closer and we pray lives will be touched and changed that day, not because of anything we have done, but because of WHO YOU ARE!"*

That same day, I cried at my own accomplishment. I walked the short length of the kitchen counter with only a cane. This walk felt more like finishing a marathon than a short indoor distance. *"God, you are so good! Thank you for helping me gain strength and accomplish new goals."*

While small gains felt huge to me, my body had a way of reminding me that I still had a long way to go. The pain in my feet and legs was relentless, so Mom prayed with me again believing for total "restoration and rebirth." The pain drove me back into bed on Sunday shortly after breakfast. That day, Mom got creative and found a way I could soak my feet in Epson Salt. The combination of her faith-filled prayers and her practical love felt like a human expression of Jesus.

The following week brought more therapy. I actually fell in therapy on Tuesday, another humbling reminder of how weak my body had become. I was thankful that it only injured my pride, but not my body. We actually had to call EMS services to assist me in getting up. Once up, I grabbed my cane and went for another walk. I knew that if I let fear settle in, my progress would be negatively impacted. I had to push into the fear and go beyond my weakness.

I actually got a real shower on Wednesday with help from the nursing aide. My dad stayed with me some days so mom could work. I was so tired after my shower that he took a nap … yes, you heard me correctly. He took the nap. That was rest enough for me, having him close by but silent. I had a good laugh over how restful this was for me.

Dinner and evening times were sweet with just my mom, but this was also a season where I struggled with an onslaught of thoughts about the days ahead. Mom would always remind me to trust in God, who had already brought me this far. We almost always ended our days praying from grateful hearts, while continuing to ask for my sight, my left side and my lungs to be supernaturally restored.

I am now at the command of everyone else's schedule and struggling with the amount of patience and perspective this requires. One therapist comes late, cutting into the next session. I have to wait for help to arrive. I cannot do the simplest of things by myself or for myself. Some days, the burden would overwhelm me to the point of sadness or depression. My blood pressure had a way of "telling on me" when my stress levels would increase. I knew I had to stay in a place of hope and peace for the sake of my health and recovery. *"Lord, help me please!"* was the constant cry of my heart. I had to remind myself that I am a grown woman, as the challenges of this season often caused me to feel trapped in a kid's body that would not cooperate and needed Mom or Dad to help. As grateful as I was for my parent's constant presence, needing them so desperately at this stage in life was also emotionally maddening. What happened to my independence? How was it stolen? Would I ever regain my ability to care for myself and live on my own?

Friday, June 27th was a good day. I had looked forward all week to having friends come over. I needed that connection to the outside world and to my former life. Mom was going out of town for the first time since my illness began. She got up early Saturday to pack and prepare. All I could do was think of a weekend with girlfriends at my side.

Mom headed out and Sarah arrived … close behind her, my father showed up. Oh well, so much for my grown up girl time. At least he brought us a good meal. I did appreciate his support but I felt at a loss for how to communicate my need to exercise some independence.

Mom called in and we prayed over the phone. I know it is hard for her to be away and feel out of control. I sense that she worries that no one will take care of me the way she does. She just may be right!

Sunday, my friend and I enjoyed a nice breakfast, entertained a few visitors, and enjoyed girl stuff like painting our nails. I felt a deep contentment that weekend.

The weekend ended abruptly as my dad arrived Monday morning at 6:20 to relieve my friend who had to go to work.

What was he thinking? He must have taken his cues from all the hospital staff that would come in and wake you just to give you a sleeping pill. I have to admit that I did wish he could relax just a bit.

The week of June 30th brought enough success with shower time that the nursing aide cut back her schedule to one time a week, leaving my other showers to me and mom. It felt like a milestone to become more and more capable of caring for myself without the assistance of professionals. This week also brought some improvement in my leg pain, so my pain medicine was reduced. I can only hope that these small gains will eventually lead me to wholeness of mind, body and spirit.

My dad would come to stay with me, then sneak outside to smoke when therapy or nursing was with me. I reminded him on Tuesday, July 1st, that he had promised to quit smoking when I could walk again. My therapist joined in on the fun, stating, *"Well, she IS walking!"*

I managed today to walk down the ramp outside with my walker, setting a goal to walk down the ramp with just a cane before my next trip out to the doctor's office. That was what my social life had been reduced to.

I was excited to see Dr. Habashi again on Thursday, July 7th. I managed to walk into her office on my walker. She was quite proud of me. She took time to educate me on how much my body needs rest and protection from germs. She said another bout of pneumonia could be fatal. She encouraged me to rest one hour in the morning and the afternoon, but to keep my eyes and hands busy the rest of the day.

As Mom and I left her office, the weight of how serious this is settled onto both of us. All we could do is hand our fear and anxiety over to God because He was the only One who could keep me safe. We delighted in re-visiting how God had kept us all free from other germs and illnesses even while exposed to many diseases in the hospital environment all those weeks. We knew He had placed a supernatural bubble of protection around us and we had to trust that this would continue. I really had to give Him my fear around flu and cold season that would accompany the change of seasons from fall into winter.

My fear gave way to tears flowing down my face as my mom confessed her fears too. But, as always, she pointed our hearts back in the direction of faith. That day reminded me that there were challenges ahead, but it also reminded me of His great love and protection to this point. That built my faith and gave me the strength to keep moving forward. Mom captured a few passages of scripture in her journal that day that became life-lines to us:

"Make thankfulness your sacrifice to God, and keep the vows you made to the Most High. Then call on me when you are in trouble, and I will rescue you, and you will give me glory." Psalm 50:14,15

"When doubts filled my mind, your comfort gave me renewed hope and cheer." Psalm 94:19

"Don't be afraid, for I am with you. Don't be discouraged, for I am your God. I will strengthen you and help you. I will hold you up with my victorious right hand." Isaiah 41:10

Mom prayed a simple, yet beautiful prayer: *"Oh God, please have mercy on Lauren. Please keep her healthy and safe. You have brought her through this far and we give you all of the praise and the glory."*

The next day was July 4th, Independence Day. Mom later told me that after our hard July 3rd, she got up ahead of me on the 4th and continued to pray: *"Lord, today is a whole new day. Thank you that we have promises in your Word to help show us the way. Fear is a horrible thing and we know it is not from You. Lord, help Lauren to have a brighter day. Thank you for her friends who give so much of their time. God, help me to be a better friend."*

Sarah, Teresa and Steve soon arrived with everything needed for a proper holiday cook-out. They even brought the grill! We ate, played monopoly and shot off fireworks. These simple pleasures were the medicine my heart needed. Mom regretted she didn't make me wear a mask all day to protect against germs. I enjoyed the freedom of being able to smile at those I love. At some point, fear had to give way to faith that God really did have this in His powerful hands. The day ended writing thank you notes with Mom … a task I could never complete!

On Saturday, the 5th, Dad brought an ultra red light wand like the one they had used while I was in Winston-Salem to reduce the pain in my feet and legs. I was most grateful for any help in dealing with this constant reminder of my new life. My parents both continued to challenge me to stay in a place of faith and hope. We all realized that my emotions would require as much restoration as my body.

Mom called me her "Dear Abby" Sunday morning after she awoke to the sound of me "counseling" a friend on the phone. During my illness, Mom would always encourage me to put myself first, but I had to remind her this time that putting myself first meant being willing to invest in others as a key part of my return to a whole life. I found it most therapeutic to re-direct my thoughts off of myself onto someone else. It felt amazing to be needed, wanted and valued. I had almost forgotten the deep sense of significance found in having something to offer.

TIME TO CELEBRATE

I had a simple outing for the first time today for a friend's special 16th birthday. I also stopped by my own apartment for the first time since January. A flood of emotions came at this season of "firsts." I was encouraged to know I could hold out physically for a simple celebration and also to know I could hold out emotionally when confronted with the losses of the past few months.

I do all I know to do … I keep applying myself to my therapy sessions. Today, I thought a lot about how grateful I am for the friends and family who surround me and keep reminding me that I will recover 100%. Eighteen people came by just today, another wave in the continuous outpouring of love that is healing me one wave at a time.

I realized that I needed to have a conversation with my parents about the importance of them giving back the reigns to my life. My high blood pressure was a reminder that my body was struggling under the weight of the transitions.

Mom captured in her journal that day, overhearing me tell a visiting friend that I would be willing to stay in a wheelchair for life if it meant one person coming to know Jesus Christ. God had given my life back. All that was left to do was give it back to Him in return, inviting Him to do with it as He desired. That simple act of surrender and faith brought much contentment and peace.

Wednesday, July 9th brought good news. I had to return to my hematologist to follow up on my white blood cell count having been too high, a sure sign of infection. He was the one who had said *"let's just wait and see"* instead of putting me through the bone marrow testing. He had felt my white cell count was high due to the unimaginable stress my body had undergone and it would take time to normalize. Today's report that my blood work was almost back to normal brought a wave of relief and joy that would be impossible to put into words. This put some much-needed wind in my sails.

Thursday marked one full month at home. I had a quiet day, with the highlight being trying on a new blouse to wear to my party. It was a perfect fit. I found myself looking forward to dressing up for a change.

Friday, July 11th was my forty-fourth birthday. Donata graciously offered to cook a birthday dinner while Sarah made plans to spend the night. My phone began ringing early with birthday wishes. Nine other friends stopped by to join in the celebration. I have to admit … I loved all of it!

We also began decorating for the "Praise the Lord" party tomorrow. A day long awaited was almost here.

Saturday arrived and over three hundred, fifty people showed up for the most amazing worship experience of my life, enhanced by delicious food prepared by our dear friends. Mom welcomed everyone and thanked them for their support. She eloquently shared about how Jesus had just seen us through the darkest time of our lives. God gave me the strength to stand with my walker and speak to this beautiful group of family and friends. I felt God speaking through both of us as we sought to bless those who had so consistently blessed us, while focusing the entire day on the One who made this day possible. Here is an excerpt from the beautiful words my Mom shared that day:

"Well, here we are six months and many, many miles later. And you have been with Lauren and this family every step of the way. This party is our way to thank the Lord and honor Him for all He has done for us. Lauren is still here with us because of God's great love and mercy – to God be the glory.

I realize there are a lot of people here who don't know each other. You have come from different parts of our lives, so introduce yourselves and make new friends. Please know that you have strengthened us with your prayers, blessed us with your love, and encouraged us with your hope. We witnessed time after time the specific ways God worked wonders through each of you. You united to show your love in many ways including:

- *Sending cards*

- *Giving us scripture to read over Lauren while she was in the coma*

- *Called, texted and sent daily emails*

- *Held fund raisers in the cold weather*

- *Sang to us*

- *Cried with us*

- *Drove us many miles to the hospitals daily*

- *Nourished us spiritually, emotionally, physically and financially*

- *Brought comfort, quiet, laughter and hugs to the waiting area*

This season would have been much more difficult without you. Sometimes, it was too difficult to talk about, so you became our voice. Thank you for allowing God to use you to minister to our family. We thank God for each of you. The most important thing you did was pray and we thank God that He honored those prayers with Lauren's life."

Mom went on to talk through the plan of salvation with the entire group in the event that someone there needed Jesus. I knew somehow deep down that this party marked the beginning of my new assignment from God, as we designed this day to encourage, bring hope, restore faith and celebrate those God has given to us. I found myself longing for the spirit of this day to define the rest of my days.

My Mom concluded by simply saying, *"There is one thing God says to every person – regardless of their circumstances – 'Trust me.' And that is our choice that we make as this journey continues. We are going to trust Him and watch Him work."* And to that, I simply said, *"Amen!"*

A NEW CHAPTER BEGINS

I felt more joy these past two days than I had felt for months combined. My birthday and this joyous party created a SHIFT within my heart. A new chapter was about to begin.

We were up until midnight in awe of this day looking at all of the cards and gifts. Everyone continued to give. I received an unbelievable amount of cards and gifts. We believed we would hear reports of how people were impacted by the day. We later heard from one woman who said she brought her children because she wanted them to know that miracles are REAL and prayer works. We were her evidence of that powerful reality, and our story had created a visual aide for her children.

Another call came on Monday from a gentleman who wanted a write-up of my story along with some pictures so he could place it in the Lincoln Herald, a local online newspaper. This marked a new chapter, a new beginning. My prayer was now being answered for my story to reach many, touch many and inspire many. I knew God was at work, as this was not something I had tried to make happen. I had simply asked God to make it happen and now people were coming our way asking to help get the story out. Mom and I both commented how fun it is to watch God at work.

Calls kept coming in from people who were blessed by our time of worship and the inspiration of the party. We quickly regretted not capturing this on video. What were we thinking?

Mom shared in her journal how she wanted me fully healed, but she also was growing fond of having me in her home. I knew that my continued improvement would create times of joy and times of painful tension as the ties that bound us through sickness would begin to be stretched by my increasing independence. We both prayed for God to lead us on His best path for both of our lives. Those two lives had become so intertwined that they almost felt like one. The challenge would be restoring them into two separate but connected lives.

Tuesday, July 15th brought another milestone. I was being evaluated to see if I qualified to transition from home health, which is for those who are unable to travel easily, to outpatient therapy. This marked a new phase of independence and mobility.

My story titled *"It Was Lauren's Day"* appeared in the Lincoln Herald's website and on their Facebook page. They included some great pictures from the party and the story was a true representation of the event and of my journey. I felt a momentum building that was divine in origin.

When Mom and I prayed that evening, we found ourselves shifting prayers from our needs to the needs of others. We focused on a friend who had a need related to her employment. This also felt like a powerful shift where my situation was coming under control enough that we could begin to look forward and cover others. This simple reality brought great joy and a sense of purpose to both of our hearts.

Mom began the week by helping reserve a local park

for our annual family picnic. Let the parties continue. I was enjoying this season of connecting with family and friends in a spirit of celebration instead of sadness. I could feel the heaviness of the past few months beginning to loose their hold on my heart. I noticed I was laughing and smiling more than I had in a long time. I was beginning to feel more like my old self. Or was it my new self?

The next few days I stayed busy with therapy, visitors and reaching out in any way possible. Thursday, July 17th was the birthday of my bestie Sarah so I decided to have balloons delivered to her office. It felt so good to have the energy to bring joy to someone else.

Just as joy would come, something would try to overshadow it. This week's particular challenge was the red tape related to getting my long term disability compensation activated. Mom's exact words were, *"What a mess!"* She then went on to echo one of her favorite lines, *"Nothin's easy anymore."*

I was released to outpatient physical therapy and our main goal was for my therapy to be completed before the onset of the new flu season. This single topic could strike fear quickly in my heart.

My day was brightened by a visit from my father and Donata. She brought me some new jewelry. Everyone knows how much I love girly things and it feels so good to begin to have energy to care about what I look like. This sweet gift was a great reminder that I am returning from the land of hospital gowns and tubes, to the realm of fashion and accessories.

By Saturday, I was exhausted again. It didn't help that I could not get comfortable in that dreaded hospital bed. I slept in while Mom cleaned the house. I needed a quiet day.

Sunday, I enjoyed a visit from Teresa while Mom shopped with my birthday money for a new iPad. Despite a good day, I found myself feeling a bit frustrated and down tonight as Mom and I came together to pray. She never seems to get tired of praying over me. She called God the calm in the middle of the storm while asking for the courage to continue to trust Him fully. I command my emotions to line up with my spirit, as I know He is still at work.

Monday, Mom became my nursing aide, helping me with my first independent shower. We did fine. No falls or catastrophes. Well, the floor did get drenched, but that would dry in no time. Then I enjoyed a quiet visit with another friend in the afternoon.

My outpatient rehab would begin on July 29th. Until then, I continued to do my home exercises for my body, my eyes and my brain. I had been given the caution to not get apathetic. Everyone told me I had to stay active all day and not give into watching TV or otherwise being passive. It was a challenge to stay motivated to do the same things day after day in a quiet house.

Friday, July 25th, Sarah and I finally got to celebrate her birthday. I was glad to have her come stay the night to enjoy pizza and some girl time. Wisely, Mom left to let us enjoy our time and to let me feel more like an adult. These fun moments made the long days of chronic pain and slow progress bearable and kept me reminded that there is life beyond these walls and someday I will rejoin that life. We were enjoying our freedom into Saturday when my dad called and insisted on bringing food by even though I assured him we had it covered. My heart sank at the feeling of being reduced to a little girl who has to obey instead of lead. I tried hard to balance gratitude with my need to have those around me understand how helpless I had felt and how much I now needed to be allowed to do anything I could without assistance. I wasn't just getting my body back … I was trying to get my life back. Being made to feel like a child could reduce me in a moment to feeling emotionally like I was back in the hospital connected to tubes and machines with no voice. I hated having decisions made for me at this stage, yet I lacked the wisdom on how to communicate my need for independence to those who were still caring for me.

Sunday, I had a long talk with a couple of friends asking them to pray for me to know how to communicate my need to be seen and heard, not controlled or dismissed.

Monday morning, Dad came by and Mom tried to express my emotional struggles with feeling like my life is not my own. He was going to wake me, but she asked him not to. He complied. He was learning and I was being honored. I slept peacefully, not realizing that my parents were still advocating for me and covering me from the other room. The way they chose to work together in this season blessed me immeasurably. My father's willingness to adapt his style of care to better suit my needs also impacted my heart deeply.

WAVE OF GRATITUDE

Thursday, July 29th finally arrived. My first day in out-patient therapy was an exciting step toward rejoining the outside world. It felt good, but exhausting, to get in the car, go for therapy and return home. I rested well from being so physically spent. Mom had battled again today with the red tape from my long term disability coverage. I was so grateful for all she was still doing to take stress off of me. I could not have handled those details along with the responsibility for my rehabilitation. Again, a wave of gratitude for family support, even though imperfect, washed over me.

Finally, on Thursday, July 31st, my disability claim was approved. This took a great weight off of my mom. I also had a great visit with Dr. Habashi. She challenged me again on the dangers of the winter flu season, and graciously agreed to come to my home to treat me if necessary. This woman's heart of compassion keeps blessing us.

We found ourselves asking for NOTHING during our prayer time, but simply thanking God for His love and presence with us. We ate take-out Mexican food and got a great night of sleep to rest up for our next party, tomorrow's family picnic.

Saturday was a clear, chilly day. It felt like crisp mountain air and we all enjoyed eating and visiting as the kids played on the near-by play ground.

Sunday, even though my body needed rest, I was a bit disappointed to have a quiet day with no one stopping by. That almost never happened, but today, it reminded me that winter would soon be here and I would have to be quarantined away from people due to the risk of catching a cold or the flu. Even though it was early August, I was already feeling a sense of dread begin to come over my heart. I quietly asked God to help me through this season. I did not want to lose faith or fall into depression.

The next day, after long hours of outpatient therapy, I went to bed exhausted only to wake and call Mom's name. I know I must have startled her into thinking something was wrong. My mind was racing around the idea of a story called *"God's Got This."* She grabbed a notepad in the middle of the night and began writing as fast as I could speak. I laid there wondering what it would be like to find a way to get my story into the hands of people who needed a life-line of hope.

This quote captures part of what my heart was musing over. *"It's important that we share our experiences with other people. Your story will heal you and your story will heal somebody else. When you tell your story, you free yourself and give other people permission to acknowledge their own story."* Iyanla Vanzant

Looking back to that time now as I am actually writing this in March of 2015, these thoughts were only seeds of faith in August 2014. God did indeed have a plan that would connect me to my co-author, a woman I would not even meet until 2015. I just knew in my heart that a story was emerging that had to be told. Now I realize that seed of desire was placed there by God and continued to be watered by my desire to bless others as I had been blessed. Yet again, I felt despair give way to faith.

Thursday, August 4th, I had to visit the doctor due to

increased leg pain. They wanted to make sure nothing new was going on, such as a blood clot. A friend had planned to come for the weekend, but had to cancel at the last moment. Mom's friend had planned to be with me Friday, but got sick. I felt like I was in an emotional battle. If I gained the slightest ground by faith, satan was right there trying to steal it. Again, I remembered John 10:10: *"A thief comes only to steal and to kill and to destroy. I have come so that they may have life and have it in abundance."* I had come too far to give in to despair.

As the evening temperatures became less hot and humid, we often found ourselves sitting at the dining room table in front of a set of open French doors. It brings perspective to enjoy God's creation in nature, to feel the wind and to soak in some evening sun. We "listen" as we sit at the table. I strain to hear what God is saying to my heart in this season.

"It's not going to be easy. It's going to be worth it." Billy Cox

"Faith is not an instinct. It certainly is not a feeling. It is an act of will, a choice, based on the unbreakable Word of a God who cannot lie." Elisabeth Elliot

"All things work together for good in the end. So if it isn't good, it isn't the end." Kris Vallotton

Sunday, August 10th marked two full months at home with no setbacks. That spoke of God's faithfulness. I am able to recognize substantial progress for my body, as I work to keep a right attitude. I enjoyed several guests over the weekend. I even received an invitation to dinner next weekend. While I have much to be grateful for, I continue to battle with chronic pain from the nerve damage. I work not to complain because I feel I have been given too much to express negativity.

In the midst of growing faith and physical improvements, I could not get death off of my mind. I asked Mom to provide stationary so I could write letters to my most valued people for her to give out if death should occur. It was a sobering time to try to focus on living while preparing if I should die. One simple cold could kill me. I couldn't escape the thought that I had probably never made it through a winter without at least one cold. Could fall or winter bring my death? If so, how should I live out this season of life?

I began to relate more to the life of Jesus, as He lived knowing the exact hour and method of His death. I pondered how He stayed focused on His mission with His ominous demise set on the horizon. If His death could bring life, He was willing to endure to the cross. Therein was my own answer. If my life could bring life to others, then it was worth staying in the game. The number of my days had less meaning now. What was important was what filled the days I had been granted. This gave me a determination to make the most of my time, pray fervently for those in my keeping and give joy and life to those with whom I visited face to face and by phone.

I knew I was internalizing part of this inner struggle, as my blood pressure was on the rise again. The doctor had to order another prescription, hoping to bring it under control. I even had to cancel a few therapy sessions as it soared dangerously high. This new complication brought fear of another stroke. This discouraged me and created a tremendous emotional battle.

The new medicine lowered my blood pressure but it also lowered my heart rate too much. When will the medical complications end? Will they end? Simple things like cutting my nails hurt due to the nerve damage. We continued to pray and Mom continued to believe for my full healing. I realize that I am holding onto faith with a fragile grip.

Later in the week another session of therapy was cancelled again due to blood pressure issues. The stress upset my stomach. I felt a bit nauseated like you feel after getting off a roller coaster. There was only one difference. This ride was not a fun thriller. It was just a thriller, absent of fun.

Saturday, August 16th, I sleep in and then prepared to enjoy dinner with one of the friends who had been so faithful during my hospitalization, often sending cards, gifts and uplifting scripture. This simple pleasure had given me something to look forward to over the past difficult week. I was able to use just a cane to go up and down stairs into her home. Mom did a little photo shoot of me outside when we returned home and proudly posted it on Facebook for our friends to see. I know she is proud. This strengthens my heart. I am trying hard ... I wonder if anyone really knows just how hard I am trying?

Monday, I am sent home yet again from therapy with my blood pressure too high. I hesitantly agreed to go to an outdoor concert with my mom. We later realized that we both went because we thought the other wanted to go. This was a lesson in the power of open and honest communication. People-pleasing was not a ditch I needed to fall into at this stage. I realize that is a pitfall for many people, especially women. I know I need to learn to be more of a God pleaser than a people pleaser. This entails seeking His voice and following His lead in every decision. I hope these lessons get etched deep into my heart as I move closer to resuming my life, as I have always had a tendency to put other's needs ahead of my own. One blessing that can come from a season where energy and resources are limited … we think more before we spend those precious resources. My hope was that these lessons would last when my resources expanded. I want to live in balance and in tune with God's leading, not just in times of crisis, but for all of my days. *"Lord, make me a person after your heart for all of my days."*

I have a few visitors over the coming days. I try to enjoy each one to the fullest before a season arrives where I am forced to limit my contact with the outside world. I gained the strength to go outside for a short distance on the walker. Despite a couple of close calls with falls, it built my confidence to be out walking in the neighborhood even if the distances were short.

Wednesday, August 20th, I am finally allowed to stay for my entire therapy sessions with my blood pressure back under control. While most would attribute this to the new medicine, I choose to give credit to my Great Physician. This entire time, Mom and I always end our evenings praying. She has never stopped placing her faith in my full recovery in Jesus, and she always encourages me to do the same. Tonight, she simply ended by saying, *"Lord, we choose to trust you. You are working."* I learned an important faith lesson from her in these days. We need to confess what we KNOW by FAITH even when our feelings don't line up.

I looked forward to a weekend of house sitting here at

Mom's while she went out of town. My cousin stayed and I was so glad to see her. She knew how to boost my confidence by acknowledging my weight loss. I admitted this was losing the hard way.

My faithful Mom wouldn't miss a prayer time, so she called and we prayed over the phone Friday night. I know her heart is still breaking over my current situation. I wonder if she realizes how much her faithful love inspires me to keep going day after day. In the words of Bill Johnson, *"We don't believe because we understand. We understand because we believe."* We both kept each other standing in a place of faith even when, especially when, we failed to understand.

Mom was back Saturday night. We rested on Sunday, played a few games, read together, enjoyed a couple of visitors, then turned in early after praying over a couple of friends who are struggling and over our nation. We both recognize that as a nation or a person moves away from the values they once held dear, they are in danger of judgment. We ask for His unconditional love and mercy to be poured out on those we love.

Monday morning, I had to rise earlier than I wanted to take a handful of medicine. I realize that this whole ordeal is allowing me to learn a sense of self-discipline that I did not fully possess. As hard as it is, I had to admit that some significant life lessons were emerging.

Tuesday, Mom knew I needed a bit of a pep talk. I was falling into the easy trap of wasting time when I could be exercising my body, my eyes and my mind. She encouraged me to use my days wisely. I was quick to tell her that I didn't want to be challenged on this anymore. I know I hurt her feelings, as she was right. As much as she was right, the battle to be on the schedule of therapists, parents, medicines and medical routines was wearing thin on my nerves.

IDENTIFYING THE REAL ENEMY

I see more clearly now how the enemy of our soul uses discouragement to beat us down when we are weary. I was exhausted from months of a routine that I had grown to dislike. I felt a bit like a prisoner who had been wrongly convicted. My body was the cell and my parents and therapists were the wardens. I loved and appreciated them, but I was longing for the freedom to make my own choices, be them positive or negative. At some point, people were going to have to let me find my way, and learn from falling if I chose to come short of my goals.

"Your Father in Heaven gets more glory out of seeing you beat the devil than He could ever get out of seeing the devil beat you." Dr. Lance Wallnau

I had to remind myself that my parents and my health care providers were not the enemy. Satan was my enemy and his desire was to see me stop short of my full potential. Why? He wants to steal any powerful testimony that would emerge out of the ashes of our struggles. I had not come this far to let him win.

"When one door closes, another opens; but we often look so long and so regretfully upon the closed door that we do not see the one which has opened for us." Alexander Graham Bell

That was the message that emerged in this season ... I

needed to stop looking back and learn to look forward, always believing that the best is yet to come.

I found myself emerging out of this fog wanting to be more positive, sharing more positive messages on Facebook and with my friends. I had no right to have an attitude toward those who had sacrificed an entire year of their lives to see me live. *"Lord, recalibrate my attitude and let me shine for you."* That was the prayer of my heart.

A good day in therapy was rewarded by four girl friends coming to visit with chocolate pie. Funny how something so small could feel so huge. And by huge, I don't mean in terms of calories. I mean in terms of joy.

I could feel God drawing near to me in this hard season, as fall was quickly approaching. The air began to hint of the coming change, as the evening breeze became crisp and cool. I ended my days thanking God for everything, the things I understood and the things I might never understand. I had to believe that in His sovereignty, they were all being used to shape my destiny.

On Friday, I was rewarded as several friends from work came with pizza to enjoy an evening of laughter and just being together. It was amazing how much joy I found in the simplest of things … a good meal, a hug, a kind word. My big weekend continued, as I actually headed out for my first theater movie on Saturday with three friends. Mom later said how much she missed having me go with her, as she needed to shop for shoes. Sunday, other friends came by to share Cherry-Lemon flavored Sundrop, a drink you might not have enjoyed unless you live in the south. For a few moments, I felt almost normal again.

BECOMING THE MIRACLE

CHAPTER 8

"If I fail, I try again, and again, and again.
If YOU fail, are you going to try again?
The human spirit can handle much worse than we realize.
It matters HOW you are going to FINISH.
Are you going to finish strong? —Nick Vujicic*

As a new week began, I actually requested for a day where no one would give me input or instructions. Despite meaning well, I realized that the requests and guidance of others was creating so much internal noise that I was having difficulty hearing my own self think. I recognized a need and was proud that I was able to communicate my needs in a positive and respectful manner. I could only hope to hold onto this new found wisdom as my independence returned.

September arrived with therapy going well. My greatest concern, along with my mom's, was my difficulty using my left hand. The stroke had affected my sensation, strength and coordination. I had to make myself incorporate a hand that felt more like it belonged to someone else into my daily activities. I found this to be quite a challenge. Our bodies seek the path of least resistance. If it is easier to just use the strong hand, it was hard to fight that instinct to include a hand that was weak and painful.

Rain fell on September 4th, and in my heart, I know this will be one of our last summer thunder storms before fall.

On Friday, the 5th, I received a dreaded report from the doctor. I was told that the stroke had been far more significant than was originally thought. He did not expect my vision to recover and he told me that may mean never driving again. My identity and independence took a hard hit with this news. He went on to say that he does not know to what degree my left side will recover. While my heart is crushed, I actually verbalized my willingness to stay in this set of circumstances if that would bring souls to Christ. Despite today's bad news, I found myself standing up from my wheelchair without any help. This simple gain was evidence that God will keep me standing when others expect me to fall. While my peripheral vision may be lost on my left side, my vision for the future is sharper than ever!

Nick Vujicic is an amazing young man born in Australia. He was born with no arms and no legs. An international speaker, husband and father today, Nick has a life of credibility behind this simple quote: *"If you can't get a miracle, become one."*

I couldn't begin to count the miracles that have accumulated, keeping me alive to this day. I was not going to give into despair even if my day of miracles ended and my day of living with what remained was beginning. Somehow, now, I had to find a balance between contentment with my current life and a bold expectation that there was more to come ... more healing, more hope, more independence, more life.

"If I could hear Christ praying for me in the next room, I would not fear a million enemies. Yet distance makes no difference. He is praying for me." Robert Murray McCheyne, Scottish Minister

The Word of God assures us that Jesus is our intercessor, always praying for us. I knew that I needed His Heavenly intercession if I was going to endure this upcoming season successfully.

I have heard it said that transition is when our mind and heart have to catch up with a change that has already taken place. As my physical progress now came much slower, I realized that my down days were simply when my mind and heart were trying to come into alignment with my new reality. That revelation gave me hope.

Mom reminded me on Sunday night that God is willing to bear our burdens for us. That wonderful promise only reinforced what He had been speaking to my heart. She reminded me to thank Him for what He has done, while praising Him for what He is still going to do. We positioned ourselves, asking God to re-write any negative medical report or self-limiting thoughts with His divine power. Jesus will have the final word ... not my body and not my doctor. It would defy practical wisdom to think I would ever drive again or live on my own. That would be the territory of the miraculous and I refused to stop short of any miracle He wanted to bring forth through me or for me.

Wednesday, September 10th, I had been home three full months. I have to admit that it felt like things should be happening much faster. Depression and anxiety continued to attack. I was sent home again from therapy due to high blood pressure. My symptoms were proof that I was holding much inside. The question was how to release those feelings in a healthy manner.

Thursday was the anniversary of 9-11. I never imagined when I visited Ground Zero that I would ever relate to the loss that those precious people experienced when the Twin Towers fell. My heart had gone out to those whose dreams were buried in the rubble. Now, I had a Ground Zero of my own. In honor of those who had lost their lives, I had only one choice. I had to choose to re-build. I could not fall short of my full natural and supernatural potential. The only way to honor those who have lost their lives prematurely is to live ours to the fullest.

Teresa visited this day and danced at our front door. This reminded me that there was more joy to come, even though I found it hard to smile and make simple decisions today.

On Friday, Mom was struggling with dizziness. It created fear to think of her not being able to help care for me. My best attempts at independence were quickly tempered with my daily need for assistance. I worried about her, but enjoyed having a friend spend some time with me over the weekend as Mom rested a bit more than usual.

Saturday, I received a visit from Pastor May and his wife, Emile. They have known me since I was a child and have remained treasured friends to our family. They brought fresh vegetables from their garden, along with a couple of inspirational books for Mom and me.

Later in the afternoon, we took a ride just to get out. Familiar places brought back fond memories. We even stopped to take pictures of a field of smiling, bright sun flowers. This flower has held significant meaning to me for years, so this sight felt like a personal touch from God.

That night, while working on my computer, I got dizzy and nauseated as my left eye began changing. For a moment my vision would improve. Then, just as quickly, it would worsen. One fear is having another stroke. I went to bed praying for God's protection and for Him to bring peace to my heart. Worrying over my own health and Mom's at the same time was almost more than my fragile heart could bear.

The next day I awoke feeling better. On one trip to the bathroom, Mom assisted me. She told me to call her when I needed her. I called her, literally, on the phone. We had a much-needed laugh. The afternoon was filled with popcorn and a movie.

The next week was filled with good blood pressure levels, good therapy sessions and quiet evenings at home with Mom. My heart was also relieved when she began feeling better. On Wednesday, when Mom picked me up at therapy, I asked her to stop by Dad's home. I showed them a video from therapy where I had walked all the way down the hall and back. This sense of accomplishment was a boost my heart really needed.

Saturday, September 20th, I made another emotional trip to my own home while running errands with Mom. It would be impossible to express what it felt like to be at my own home less than five times since January. Everything was still in its place collecting dust. My life felt a bit like that ... most everything was now back in place, but my pace had been slowed so much that I felt fearful of "collecting dust" so to speak. I was beginning to long for more purpose, more independence and more life. While I tried hard to be grateful for every visit, every outing, and every gain, the simplicity of my current existence was beginning to wear thin.

TIME TO BUY A LIMO AND HIRE A DRIVER

The following week, the neurologist stated I would never drive again. Mom and I quickly commented that the final decision was up to God. We even shared about Jesus with the receptionist. It felt good to share the One who had brought me this far. On the way out of his office, I lightly quipped, "Well, that settles it. I will just have to buy a limousine and hire a driver." I had learned along the way that my perspective held the power to immediately reframe hard news into a new opportunity to exercise faith and hope.

Mom headed out of town for an event, and I had to dig deep to be gracious to others staying with me who knew less about my routine. It was hard enough to allow my own mother to help me with personal care. My dignity took a harder hit when that responsibility fell onto others in her absence. As always, she continued to call every night to read with me, pray with me and encourage me. I just wanted her to come home. My heart rested when she returned Saturday evening early to surprise me. I was secretly glad that no immediate trips were planned. I needed her more than I wanted to admit. She brought far more than physical assistance. She brought courage, faith and joy to my days.

Monday, September 29th marked another week in therapy and another milestone, transitioning from the walker to a cane. I had an MRI and an MRA on Tuesday to further assess the damage to my brain. I made it through this calmly, a gift from God. I was glad to get home from Charlotte to enjoy a home cooked meal delivered by a friend, complete with apple pie.

October arrived as I awaited the results of the new tests. We filled weekends with drives and movies at home. It was mostly me and Mom in this season. While we enjoyed each other, this season was not without its challenges. Mom had to manage my life for me. In addition to my personal care, this included managing insurance, medicines, finances, social activities, doctor visits and transportation. I struggled again with feeling like a child, while she struggled trying to help me get through this. We felt stress for a few days, until God reminded us that we were giving the enemy room to enter in.

On Wednesday, October 8th, we drove to Charlotte for the results of my neurological tests. While the doctor showed us evidence that my stroke was much larger than first believed, my chances of another stroke was minimal as my critical illness had brought this one on. That took a huge weight of stress off of my mind.

The weekend was quiet. I watched black birds out the back window, watched movies, visited with Mom and napped. The atmosphere had less stress and we were both grateful for that. On Sunday, Mom started reading me some of the journal entries she had kept meticulously while I had been so sick. She still records the details of every day. She said she is afraid to stop, fearing a detail captured might once again save my life.

Reading them together was an emotional experience, but it was also healing to our hearts to realize once again how far I had come. It made me realize how much I wanted to turn this story into a book ... a dream I did not know if I would ever realize.

We worked on a jigsaw puzzle and I tried to practice picking each piece up as an extension of my left hand therapy. I quietly resented how every little thing had to be turned into therapy. I looked forward to the day when I could do simple things just because.

The next few days passed quietly with more therapy and quiet living. On Friday, I was even able to walk some outside holding onto my father instead of my cane. This felt like a picture, that as I continue to hold only my Heavenly Father, He will continue to take me further into my full recovery. In these slow days with far too little to occupy my mind, I had to believe!

Over the weekend Mom took great care to make the time fun in light of the fact that I was now cut off from people. We took a drive to get fall apples and purchased supplies to do a craft project. We picked up take-out for dinner. The air was cool and crisp, leading into Sunday. Somehow, I managed to pull a muscle, so the day was spent in pain. I watched Mom sit outside and talk to her friend. This caused me to feel cut off from life. We both felt down.

Monday, October 10th brought another day of therapy and another day of pain. The pain in my hip was worse today from the pulled muscle and it made me dread therapy. My therapist felt I should have a nerve conduction study to further investigate the cause of the numbness that was limiting the coordination of my left side.

Tuesday, Mom was able to begin working from home for the winter. It was comforting to know that I would not have to spend those days alone.

The day passed again quietly with therapy, dinner and prayer time with Mom. While our faith is strong, our emotions are heavy. We both feel the heaviness of my slow progress and ongoing challenges of chronic pain weighing me down.

This week, Mom and I decided to read a new book titled *Crazy Love* by Francis Chan. This powerful little red book takes the reader on a wild ride away from traditional religion into the heart of God to confront the cross and the truth that without love, this faith journey is nothing. We are called to love. This was good news. I could still love. Here are a few quotes that captured my heart:

"God doesn't call us to be comfortable. He calls us to trust Him so completely that we are unafraid to put ourselves in situations where we will be in trouble if He doesn't come through."

"Has your relationship with God changed the way you live your life?"

"When it's hard and you are doubtful, give more."

"We never grow closer to God when we just live life. It takes deliberate pursuit and attentiveness."

"Gods definition of what matters is pretty straightforward. He measures our lives by how we love."

In this new season, it felt as if Frances Chan was eavesdropping on the deepest desires of my heart. I slowly began to realize that this fall and winter season just may be an invitation to deliberately pursue more of Jesus in the quiet of the days. Most of us spend our days intentionally filling our calendars to overflowing. We want to be busy then turn around and complain about being too busy. We find ourselves saying things like, *"I just don't have enough time."*

What would happen if I could begin to view the slow pace and quiet as a gift in which I might encounter more of God's heart toward me. While I do not believe, as many do, that God crafted this suffering for me, I do believe fully that He was powerful enough to bring great purpose, growth and contentment from it. While I attribute my sickness to the hand of our adversary, satan himself, I held tightly to the belief that Jesus had rescued me from his hand and was lifting me to a higher place in Him.

One thing that happened in therapy this week after they discovered one leg was significantly shorter than the other was a procedure which brought my hips and pelvis back into alignment. It made the pain even worse for a few days, but my therapist assured me this would stop the hip and back pain I had been experiencing.

I saw a spiritual parallel in this. God was bringing alignment to my heart by showing me His heart. His heart was to draw me closer, so close that I could hear His heart beat. If I could get that close, I would be able to discern what He wants to bring out of this painful season of my life. This new perspective of His unending love toward me and His desire to quietly pursue me completely overwhelmed me. This realization set me on a path toward His deeply personal *"Crazy Love"* for me.

Think about it. No matter how busy anyone is, when someone comes along who has the potential to become a lover as in an intimate husband/wife relationship, we make time to pursue them and get to know them. We may even shut out the world, ceasing to spend as much time with those in our daily circle of relationships. Perhaps this season for me could be put into that framework. Jesus was pursuing me for a deeper relationship, and while the aligning did bring the pain of isolation, it also brought the joy of intimately relating to the One who had rescued me.

What if He rescued me from death just so He could live with me? What if this was all about Him wanting to see my potential un-fold? What if this was about Jesus wanting to bring life to others through our love relationship and through His Spirit pouring out of me onto those around me?

What if my survival was not about ME at all? I was beginning to see through His eyes of love that this was about JESUS and His desire to bring His love and an awareness of His character to others through my story. This revelation brought peace like a river to my soul.

On Friday, Mom and I continued reading her journals together. I cried and I know my emotion makes this hard for her. As she would read, some parts would feel strangely familiar to me. This was causing more memories to return. As painful as it was, I also knew this was a healing journey. The flood of memories made for a sleepless night, so I suggested not reading the next day. It was almost as if my heart was directing this journey one day at a time.

I was tired on Saturday, but found the energy to Facetime with a friend, using the video capacity of my cell phone to make the connection feel more like a face to face visit. I also took a ride with Mom. A friend brought by some treats with the fall theme. I found joy in these little things while still feeling a bit overwhelmed by the memories that were resurfacing.

Sunday was a quiet day over a lazy breakfast with the French doors open to the warm fall sun, happy movies (I think Mom is afraid I can't handle any sad movies), and taking time to write a few more thank you notes. My Mom stays positioned daily to bless me, serve me and pray with me. She prays daily for my full healing. Her faith and presence in this season brought more joy and life than she probably realized.

Monday, October 27th marks another week of therapy and working toward regaining my independence. A new goal is to be mobile enough and safe enough that I can spend a night home alone. I love the idea of being able to do my own thing, even if just for a few hours with no one else present. I had been used to living alone and so had Mom. I knew we were both ready for that break to come.

I actually enjoyed therapy in this season because it felt directly related to regaining my independence. I was overjoyed to have lost a few more pounds and found myself getting closer to walking without assistance.

I tried to stay focused on working out, walking as much as possible, riding my home exercise bike daily and making good food choices. It felt like I was in training. The question still remained. What was I training for? Where would this road lead?

My father was also a great coach in this season, often coming by to visit and help out with my therapy. He really enjoyed pushing my workouts to the next level, sometimes too hard. While I may have complained on occasion, I was grateful to realize that he believed in me and my ability to excel.

Almost daily, Mom and I find ourselves sitting in front of the open French doors remarking how we no longer take nature and creation for granted. I now notice small things that I used to ignore. She said the same was true for her. I feel as if I was awakened to a new level of awareness and the slowness of this season helped to reinforce that willingness to really see the blessings around us.

Friday, October 31st was Halloween. The staff at rehab dressed up as M & M characters in my honor. Fun, fun, fun! This made me laugh. We turned it into a photo shoot and I looked forward to posting pictures so my friends could see what I was up to. I remember remarking to Mom on the way home that this was my best Halloween ever. The day wore me out, giving me the gift of a peaceful night of sleep. To sleep through any night was still an answer to prayer, as the dark often reminded me of the coma and my darkest days. I wondered if that curse would ever be lifted.

November 1st brought the time change associated with Daylight Savings Time. I dreaded the early dark evenings. We heard it snowed in the mountains nearby as winter had arrived. The day was spent resting, watching movies, playing games. The weekends are now a must for my body to recover from the therapy and fatigue that comes from working hard throughout the week. Simple daily activities now make me feel as if I have run a marathon.

I find myself worrying that Mom's life is being too disrupted by this season. She remains faithful, present and full of faith. That faith pours out every night as prayers for my full recovery flow from her endlessly. I marvel at her strength and at her willingness to have her life put on hold so my life can begin again. C.S. Lewis once said, *"Hardships often prepare ordinary people for an extraordinary destiny."* If this was true for me in this season, it must also be true for Mom. Where would this lead both of us? What would ultimately come out of this season of change?

Another quote really captures my heart toward my mom. *"How we walk with the broken speaks louder than how we sit with the great."* Bill Bennot I was being allowed to see selfless love, faith, endurance, strength and patience in my own mother that made me want to possess all of these qualities in my own life. She had quietly and slowly become one of my greatest heroes, and this week, that reality settled deep into my spirit as I continued to live with her, pray with her and enjoy our time together every day.

Monday was just another day in therapy but that evening something frightening occurred. I suddenly began to feel my heart racing and I felt as if I was going to pass out. I decided to go to bed early and try to sleep it off. Mom told me the next day that she stayed awake watching over me. She went on to tell me that my breathing was erratic just as it had been all those days in the hospital. My heart aches for her as I realize this incident caused her to relive the pain of those days emotionally.

I VOTED IN MY PAJAMAS

Regardless of the emotional roller coaster we were riding, day to day life did not stop. Tuesday was Election Day. I actually got to go and vote curbside in my pajamas. I felt better with no other symptoms and the crisis passed on its own.

The hospital bed is so uncomfortable, but much easier to get into and out of as it is adjustable. I just have to learn to get in and out of a regular bed. I am ready for this next step. My body is screaming to get off that terrible mattress so I ask Mom if I can sleep part of the night in her bed.

The days blur into another round of therapy, meals, movies and talking to friends by phone. I look forward to the upcoming weekend, as Mom agreed to take me to my home to pick up some of my Christmas decorations for a bit of early decorating here at her home.

On Monday, November 11th, I shocked Dad by meeting him at the door to let him in. He grabbed me and hugged me. I continued this little independent streak by getting myself dressed for therapy on my own. I rewarded myself on the way home from therapy with a little shopping to purchase a new hand bag and wallet. Mom brought a selection of Vera Bradley hand bags out to the car so I could choose.

The next day, Mom got worried when I met a guy on Facebook. I had to laugh at the absurdity of her concern. He was from Germany and I was fairly sure that I wouldn't be flying internationally any time soon. We had a good laugh about it.

Wednesday, I stood almost two hours in therapy doing a variety of tasks designed to gain strength and endurance. After getting home, I headed to the refrigerator to get myself a cold drink. Mom and I had another good laugh about how much progress I could make if she behaved more like a therapist, training me to do things on my own instead of being so quick to do them for me. I was so exhausted at the end of the busy day that my joints ached, especially my ankles. Dad ended my day by bringing over a small table designated for puzzles and games.

Friday, November 14th, I had to get up early to have blood work done. We stopped by the grocery store on the way.

I had been concerned about losing my cosmetology license since I had been unable to attend continuing education classes. This day, I learned that I was allowed to do my classes online, along with studying a series of videos and paying a fee to renew the license. Now my license would have to be renewed every three years and no more continuing education would be required. This overjoyed me to realize that I would not lose what I had worked so hard to achieve. It felt good to have an accomplishment related to something other than my therapy. This milestone professionally was a boost for my morale.

Mom and I enjoy a quiet day Saturday, as she planned a day away with her friends on Sunday. She later remarked how she is miserable when she is away from me. I encouraged her to go, as I realize that she must sustain her friendships so she will have support when I am able to return home. She says that I am her world and she's so thankful I am alive. I don't know how to tell her, but I want her world to be so much larger than just me. My heart aches when I see that her world has been reduced to taking care of me. It actually frightens me to realize how content she seems in that role. How will we both adjust to life after this season together? I pray that we will know how to love and honor each other through that transition when the time comes.

Therapy and cosmetology videos were the pinnacle of my excitement in this season. Being so housebound was beginning to wear thin on my emotions. My body ached all over. I was trying to make the best of these days, but keeping a good attitude was not easy. It added to my frustration to be able to see the pain in my mom's eyes as she watched me struggle.

For the first time in a while, I had to cut therapy short due to high blood pressure and a headache. In part, I may have been feeling anxiety over my upcoming nerve conduction test to be done the next day. While I wanted answers as to what was causing the numbness and pain in my body, I was almost afraid of what the tests might reveal.

The day of the scan arrived, Thursday, November 20th. The results were neuropathy (damage to my nerves) that had most likely been caused by sustained bed rest and the extreme assault on my body from the critical illness. The doctor said that nerves heal slowly and it could take up to three years to know if they will heal or if the damage will be permanent. The test awakened a new level of pain in my nerve endings. I hurt all afternoon as a constant reminder of what had just taken place and the toll this year had taken on my body. I did manage to sleep all night in a regular bed for the first time. I needed that accomplishment in light of the test results and knowing it could take years to know if my body would recover.

On Friday, I headed for an appointment with Dr. Habashi. It is always emotional seeing her, as I know she saved my life and I have impacted hers. She told us that a woman from the first hospital recently asked if Lauren had died. Dr. Habashi proudly reported, *"No, she walks into my office regularly."* I was so grateful for her expertise and for her compassion. She always had a way of making me believe that I would go further and accomplish more than most of the other medical staff.

She changed my medicine and ordered some further testing. Before I left her office, she relayed a story I had not heard. One day she was with me when my vitals were unstable and she saw a tear fall from my eye. She said she felt in her heart that I thought I was going to die. She determined in that moment to pray, *"Oh Lord, please don't let me lose her."* As she prayed, my vitals normalized. In that moment, I was more aware than ever of what a huge investment this precious woman made to my recovery. She allowed God to converge her faith with her medical skill, creating a powerful combination that contributed immeasurably to my survival.

Upon arriving home exhausted, I lay down to take a nap ... but I didn't fall asleep until I took time to thank God once again for the gift of this amazing doctor. She was a gift to us from the Great Physician Himself.

The next day, November 21st, was Mom's birthday. I had fun making her a home-made card that looked like I was in the fifth grade. I included the lyrics to a favorite song that reminded her she is my hero. Friends brought our dinner while my dad brought a blood pressure cuff. No matter how much we tried to enjoy life, there were always painful reminders of the fact that I was still not totally out of the woods.

We both found ourselves exhausted for no reason, so we headed to bed early and slept all night. I was always thankful for the simple gift of a great night of sleep.

Sunday, we were invited to Teresa's church to pick up Thanksgiving meals that they were providing for the community. The rain made it a good day for a warm meal and a Christmas movie. We both had grateful hearts as we turned in for the night.

Monday brought yet another milestone. I stayed home alone for a few hours before Dad arrived to take me to therapy. He remarked that he would have come early if he knew I was alone. I quietly thought, *"That's exactly why I didn't tell you I was alone."* It felt amazing to manage on my own, even if it was just a few short hours. I felt my confidence going to the next level.

On Tuesday, I remarked to Mom while sitting around resting that I felt like just getting up and walking normal. She quickly said, *"Well then, just do it."* I stood up and walked three laps around the house with no assistance. The words of Andy Stanley ring in my heart: *"Your greatest contribution to the Kingdom of God may not be something you do, but someone you raise."* Mom's comment was so simple, but it echoed a deeper reality. She was beginning to let go, while challenging me to move beyond the place where limitations had held me captive. I could only hope in those moments that this amazing woman realized the size of her impact on my recovery, emotionally and physically. I went on to pray that as God began to use my life again, she would see that it would not have been possible if it had not been for her steadfast love.

HOME ALONE

Wednesday, I stayed home alone again for a few hours. Mom battled with insurance to get the MRI approved that my doctor and therapists felt was needed to determine why use of my shoulders caused my hands to go numb. They would only approve an x-ray before an MRI could be done.

Another friend invited us to come by tomorrow, knowing I could not come in, and grab take-out plates of their Thanksgiving meal. Our day ended with hearts full of gratitude.

Thursday arrives. I have never had more to be thankful for than I do this year. We took a drive to pick up the food that our friends had offered to share. We ate so much lunch that we barely needed any dinner. We asked for nothing during our prayer time … we just thanked Jesus for who He is to us and for all the ways He encourages and sustains us.

Friday is the day for decorating the tree for Christmas. We laughed after I wanted to get a photo of Mom's wreath she had placed on the door. She headed outside to snap the shot, not realizing that the photo captured her legs and flip flops sticking out beneath the wreath. We had a good laugh and we sat back to enjoy the beauty of our creation. Predictably, we watched a Christmas movie that night.

We took a ride the next day to run some errands. This included a stop by my home, which always brings up mixed emotions. Once back to Mom's, I had fun wrapping a few Christmas gifts. I know Mom doesn't love doing this, so I appreciated her efforts to make it a fun activity we could enjoy together. Mom and I actually walked out the driveway and down past the neighbor's home with only my cane.

December comes and I spend one of my first full days alone on the 3rd. I worked most of the day completing educational requirements to renew my cosmetology license. It would be almost impossible to describe what it felt like to be able to mark this milestone. Days like this gave me hope that I would be able to live alone again someday, even if I did not know when that day would come.

Thursday, I ended up working out at home again on my own because my dad had planned to be with me but had to cancel because he was sick. I really enjoyed my time alone but was concerned about my dad being sick and also quietly concerned because I had been around him. The fear of catching a cold or virus gripped my thoughts. I prayed to not get sick and I prayed for him to quickly get well.

Friday, I had rehab for hours then came home to begin writing Christmas cards. What a joy to be able to participate in simple traditions again. My co-workers included me in a conference call as they held their annual Christmas ornament party, where I got to choose a gift, a beautiful wooden Christmas tree. While I missed being able to be there face-to-face, I did feel loved and included.

Saturday was a quiet and rainy day. Mom and I chose to stay in and watch Christmas movies. Afterwards, we got out an old hymnal and sang some of the wonderful old songs of faith. A new wave of gratitude washed over me in the midst of this season of house arrest that reminded me that I survived for a reason and by choosing to walk by faith, that reason would be manifest in the days to come.

Sunday, I listened to a minister on TV. His message was about "waiting on God's timing." This was a timely reminder that He is going with me into the future that I cannot see fully. Mom and I drove to Hickory and got to see Sarah from a distance. I was unprepared for how it would affect me emotionally to see all of the people out freely making Christmas plans, shopping, decorating, and celebrating. When we reached my own apartment, the tears began to fall. Mom quietly encouraged me and the heaviness of my heart lifted somewhat. We headed back home, taking time to drive slowly through several neighborhoods adorned with lights. I was reminded that His light shines best in the darkness, and that His light even holds the power to dispel the darkness. I grabbed hold of a key for keeping hope alive in my heart in this season, and that was to stay connected to the source of Light, Jesus Himself.

Monday, December 12th, I needed that light more than I had in a long time. I awoke with the initial signs of getting sick. My voice was cracking and my sinuses were congested. I called Mom at work and she heard it in my voice immediately. She headed straight over to Dr. Habashi's office to ask her advice. This precious woman who had once been used by God to save my very life said something sobering. *"Meet me here at 2:15. We have to treat this aggressively and that will require admitting Lauren to the hospital."*

I was admitted to room 230 almost as quickly as I arrived. Medical staff began intervening as if it was life and death. Blood work was done quickly to test for flu. An IV was started in my arm. My congestion worsened in my sinuses, ears and head, so the doctor started antibiotics and steroids to try and keep it confined there and out of my fragile lungs. The day continued on with an EKG, cultures, x-rays, and a whole new cocktail of medicines to swallow.

This was unimaginable. How did this happen? How did I get sick after being so careful? Would they be able to keep this from spreading to my lungs?

One particular nurse came in and remembered me from my initial hospitalization. She was shocked I had survived. This simple encounter reset my focus off of my current situation back onto the God who had delivered me from near death almost a full year ago. Mom and I prayed, placing our faith in Him to bring me out of this quickly and with no setbacks in my overall health. I had to believe!

Mom spent a restless night with me. A severe headache kept me from resting. Mom directed the activities from the sidelines of my hospital bed, joking that she thinks she has the staff well trained. Dr. Habashi intervened and ordered new medicine to control my sinus headache. The flu test came back negative, which was great news. The conclusion was that I had an upper respiratory infection. She wanted me to eat some real food and stay out of bed as much as possible. Her presence and this good news brought calm to the room that allowed me to slip into a peaceful afternoon nap. She also ordered an MRI to check on my ongoing complaints about my shoulder and back pain. She said the findings could help direct the therapists in my rehabilitation.

The night was restless with all of the activity that makes it impossible to sleep in a hospital unless you ARE in a coma. I was already looking forward to being back home in the quiet. I had to laugh at the incongruity of my own thoughts. I was now longing for the quiet that had been making me feel so isolated and crazy just a few days ago. I had my own inner laugh at how discontent humans are much of our lives, always wanting what we don't have and not wanting what and who we do have. I prayed that I would come out of this ordeal more at peace and rest with my own circumstances.

A fire alarm went off and we were told to stay in the room. Mom assured the nurses that she was working out her PLAN in case it turned out to be a real emergency. They all had a good-hearted laugh at her take-charge nature. While it might frustrate some, even me at times, I was reminded that her strategic thinking and her strong will had been used by God to keep professionals on their toes as they worked to save my life. I told her how grateful I was for her and how sorry I was for anything I had done to make this journey harder for her. That was part of the agony of this season. My bad days did not simply affect me. They spilled over onto those that had to be present to assist me. My days were no longer my own and I felt guilty for any way I had stressed or hurt her. She assured me I had done fine and just to rest. I realized that this new visit to the hospital was triggering many emotions from former weeks.

The MRI took a couple of hours. I had hopes that it would reveal a cause of some of my residual pain so it could be treated. Another nurse came to my room and recognized me from before, stating, *"Wow. You really have a testimony."*

Revelation 12:11 says, *"They conquered…by the blood of the Lamb and by the word of their testimony."*

I now realized that I had been brought back into this hospital setting and God was using it to remind me that a testimony began in this setting and that I had overcome by the power of His blood healing me. He then reminded me that I would continue to overcome and gain strength as I spoke out what He had done. A testimony is like seed. When we speak out what God is doing and has done, we sow those seeds of hope and life into the heart of the one who is hearing. That in turn has the power to bring transformation and new life to others.

My heart settled into complete peace. He had seen me through far more serious circumstances. I knew now I could just rest and let His presence bring me through this new situation. It would not defeat me. It would only add another layer to my testimony and I was more determined than ever to let that story bring life to others.

My spirit was strong but my emotions were weak. The medicine that controlled my leg pain had to be stopped during the antibiotics. The pain was making it hard to rest. The MRI didn't show anything that would really change the course of my treatment. I had to work hard to hold onto hope. I felt the roller coaster of emotions start up again, strong one minute and weak the next.

Friday was a frustrating day. I awoke with a sore throat which sent the staff into frenzy. They said they would call Dr. Habashi that morning. At 1:30 pm, Mom learned that she had not been called as a nurse had taken the authority to determine that the medication I was on was sufficient. As you know by now, she and Mom were about to have a meeting. Warrior Mom came out in full force and things started happening on my behalf. Again, it overwhelmed us to wonder how anyone manages without an advocate. We had a good laugh when I told Mom that I bet she wished she was an octopus. She asked why and I said so she could slap eight people at the same time. The thought wasn't sanctified but it was honest and the laughter broke the tension. As we were laughing, the automatic paper towel dispenser made a loud noise and activated, spitting out a paper towel. We laughed even harder.

Saturday, December 13th was a day I will never forget. After only a few short days in the hospital, I was GOING HOME! I was not totally well, but they felt I was well enough to finish my medication and recover at home. They actually said they wanted to release me before I caught more germs by being in the hospital.

I went home and got right in the shower to rid my

body of those germs. Our prayer time that night focused on thanking God for the miracle of this infection staying out of my lungs. I was so grateful to be home and to be under the watchful eye of Jesus ... and Warrior Mom.

Sunday, I was grateful to be home but the medicines were making me feel terrible. The steroids made me feel jumpy on the inside and caused hot flashes. The pain in my legs was far worse since I still couldn't take all of my medicines. I watched Christmas movies trying to distract myself from how I was feeling.

I didn't miss a beat in therapy, an answer to prayer. Monday morning, I was right back at the gym. While I still was not feeling up to par, it felt good to return to my routine. Therapy always made me feel I was moving forward and progressing.

All I could do over the coming days was trust. The steroids would end on Friday. That gave me hope of returning more to normal. Cards of encouragement poured in and I was so grateful for those who stood with me and my family.

Wednesday, December 17th, I did something I had not been able to do for almost a year. I tied my own shoes and I felt like the kid in the song, *"All I want for Christmas is my two front teeth."* I could think of a long list of simple things I could substitute for that kid's two front teeth. The quiet longing to have the simple things returned that I felt had been stolen gripped my heart. On one hand, it felt almost selfish to ask for anything more since God had given my life back. But I still couldn't help but long for that life to now return back to normal. Just like the kid who wanted those two teeth back to fill the empty hole, I longed for a more complete healing in my body so the holes left by house arrest, isolation and weakness could be filled again with friends, celebration, work, and meaningful activities. I was alive and yet I missed living ... really living.

It felt odd to spend part of the next two days helping Mom get gifts ready for family and friends who would come by to pick them up. I felt so cut off from all of the Christmas joy associated with being with the ones you love.

I learned on Friday that my co-workers had selected me for their angel tree donation. I marveled again at how my friends from work and from life had rallied around me, adding much joy and hope to this season of life. In my book, they were the angels. Not me.

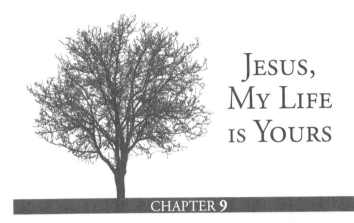

Jesus, My Life is Yours

CHAPTER 9

"You can make many plans,
but the Lord's purpose will prevail."
—Proverbs 19:21

Saturday, December 20th brought a morning in the kitchen finishing cookies and snacks that would be picked up in the afternoon for Mom's family Christmas celebration. The food and gifts were sent and when the family was together, they Facetimed us so all of the family members could share a personal message with us. What a joy this was as we could not attend due to my quarantine. Several hours later, the doorbell rang. We were amazed to see the entire family standing in our front yard singing Christmas songs to us. They all wore Santa hats and huge smiles. Mom and I both needed this boost of joy. While we couldn't give hugs or invite them in, we felt them with us throughout the evening as we enjoyed those great memories while dining on food they had prepared for us and opening the gifts they had brought.

In the quiet of the night, I thought of Mary and Joseph

all alone as Jesus was born. They were denied a place to rest, having to settle for a barn full of smelly animals. Here I was in the comfort of my own mother's home, recovering successfully from this recent setback while surrounded by the not-so-distant love of my family and friends. A few men finally found their way to Jesus, bringing gifts of honor. Countless gifts of blessing and honor had been poured out on us during this hard season. It made me reflect on how much I wanted to now offer my life as my gift, reminding Jesus that He could do with it and with me whatever He desired from this season forward.

This Christmas spent separated from those I loved was doing a deep work in my heart. It made me think of how Jesus was born with a destiny of death as the sacrifice that would unleash His ultimate destiny. Restoration to God for us would have never been possible if He had forsaken His call to death and resurrection. For almost a year, I did not know if I would live or die. Jesus knew all along that His death was inevitable. Yet, the Word of God tells us that He endured to the cross because of the joy that was set before Him. I believe the joy that kept Him faithfully moving toward His cross His entire life was the joy of knowing that some would choose out of love to follow Him there, laying down their lives in exchange for the life He wants to live through us.

UNLEASH RESURRECTION POWER

I had followed Jesus to His cross and had died with Him, not because of H1N1 flu, but because I chose to embrace salvation. I fully believe that, at the time of salvation, my life was buried in death with Christ and that His life was then awakened within me as He was resurrected. In other words, my old self died at the cross and it is now Jesus who lives in and through me. My laid-down life is the gift I bring to Him this Christmas, reminding Him and reminding myself that He is now invited to fill me to overflowing with the same power and purpose that drove Him to the cross – and beyond – so that my story, my life and my love for Him could unleash resurrection power in those around me.

Jesus was born to die so that you and I can be born again to live. Marianne Williamson once said, *"Something very beautiful happens to people when their world has fallen apart: a humility, a nobility, a higher intelligence emerges at just the point when our knees hit the floor."*

The events of this past year drove me to my knees. There I was positioned much like the first men who arrived at His birth ... they offered their gifts and they fell on their knees to worship Jesus, their Messiah. I could only hope that the simple gift of my life and the worship of my heart would bless Him. I wanted His birth, His death and His resurrection to all be honored by my life. I wanted the joy that He saw as He looked forward past His own cross to be found in my smile, in my attitude, in my faith and in my heart during this season when life weighed heavy like a death sentence. If I were to crush an orange peel in my hand, it would release the oil from the skin and the fragrance of that orange would fill the air. It became my prayer for my life to release the fragrance of gratitude, joy and honor back to Heaven as a thank offering as I was being crushed by the weight of these trials and tests.

Romans 15:13 promises us this. *"Now may the God of hope fill you with all joy and peace as you believe in Him so that you may overflow with hope by the power of the Holy Spirit."*

There was another key. My simple acts of faith, when fueled by the power of the Holy Spirit, would unleash joy and peace as I chose to keep releasing my future to Him. I don't want anyone to think I did anything special. I want every reader to take hold of that last phrase in this verse to realize that my faith during this season was a gift from the Holy Spirit who empowered me to overcome. It was not that my faith was great … His power was great. In fact, His power is so great that this joy and peace were promised to overflow out of my life and into yours. My new desire is for Jesus to overflow out of me daily in ways I never dreamed possible.

Then another amazing reality hit me. If I died with Jesus at the cross, I am already dead … so the fear of death to come is only an illusion. As a daughter of God, my life is now hidden with Jesus as I wait to be reunited with Him in Heaven at the time that my earthly body gives way to a new glorified body. All that's left is gain when we place our trust in Him.

Christmas came and went quietly in the sanctuary of my mom's home. Even though we were somewhat isolated, we could feel the love flowing to us from our family, our friends and from the Throne Room of Heaven.

Kris Vallotton once said, *"Love rewrites your history."* Jesus' love for me and for you at the cross rewrote our history. Our lives now have a destiny that connects us to the greater story of His plan to redeem the world to Himself. We have a choice to make. Will we choose to stay on our own self-directed path or will we choose to lay ourselves at His feet to receive His new blueprints for our future?

Even though I would have called myself a person of faith before I got so sick, I would now have to admit that I was living a self-guided life, doing mostly what I wanted with my independent life. I worked where I wanted, befriended who I wanted, hung out alone at home or with company when I wanted.

Now, life is going to be different. This crushing has produced an awareness that my life is not my own. I have been bought with a price and that price cost Jesus His own life. The cost associated with this season has been great. My illness has cost me my ability to live independently. It has cost me my freedom of mobility. It has now cost me my job, as I just learned that my one year leave of absence has expired.

Yes, a full year has passed. I am still on house arrest due to my fragile immune system. My doctor says that will likely last until late spring. I cannot see my friends or my family. I cannot go to church or to a movie. I cannot drive my own car due to my loss of vision. I cannot go to the mall with a friend.

My past year looks like a long list of losses. It may look like death. But look closer.

Jesus was crucified, buried and presumed dead only to be found having escaped a sealed tomb. The rest of that story is still unleashing resurrection power to all who choose to believe. HIS TOMB IS EMPTY!

And thanks to His resurrection power, my TUNNEL IS EMPTY! I feel a bit like a butterfly coming out of the cocoon. I have emerged into the light of day and I am more determined than ever to allow Jesus full access to my life. Jesus lives and He brought me back from the brink of death to echo His saving power. I am alive and I will shout from any rooftop I can find that my life is of great value and I will emerge victorious. The end of this story has not yet been told.

I now plan to follow Jesus as He leads me on what work I commit to, who I connect with and how I spend my days. There is a lot of uncertainty ahead for me as I await the signal that I am free to leave this house and head out into life. But I know one thing for sure now. I have nothing to lose and everything to gain. I can echo the thoughts of motivator, Darrin Hardy as he says, *"Approach your goals like this, 'This is my mountain, and I'm going all the way to the top! You are either going to see me waving from the summit or lying dead on the side. I am not coming back!'"*

I have learned one thing for sure. I could have easily died at 43. Whether 43 or 83, life is short and how we spend our days may count more than we think. Elite athletes have been cresting Mount Everest and other major mountains for years. They often plant a flag at the summit. Well, I am about to plant my own flag of sorts at the summit. I am now humbled and grateful to hold my survivor flag high overhead.

MY SECRET SPRING MISSION

You are holding a book in your hands. It represents my one-year journey.

One of my favorite sporting events of all time now feels like the book ends on either side of this season, start and finish.

At the time of the 2014 Super Bowl, I was in a coma fighting for my life.

At the time of the 2015 Super Bowl, played on February 1st, I was happy to be alive to watch the game with my own mom while still isolated from the crowd. She knows nothing about football, which made me feel like the resident expert. I tried to explain the game almost play by play, returning the favor where my Mom had relayed the events of the months I lost while in a coma almost play by play from her daily journals. I even got to influence her as to which team we were pulling for. Again, this reminded me of how Mom had single-handedly determined that my fight for life was going to align with God's perfect plan. She placed her entire life on hold to join me in this fight. When game day came, we just had fun pulling for the team of our (my) choice. It felt like an amazing gift to know this day was not guaranteed this time last year. But it had come to pass nonetheless.

Around the time that the 2015 game aired, Mom found a magazine in her home. She had never seen one before and did not know where it came from. Upon reading some of the articles, she felt compelled to call the owner to inquire if she knew anyone who might be willing to help make my dream of telling this story possible. One phone call later, I was connected to Kim Fletcher, my co-author and friend. When Mom and I discussed the path that led us to Kim recently, we realized that Mom made that first phone call on January 14, 2015, exactly one year to the day from when I first went into the hospital. Kim returned her call that same day.

Five months later, the manuscript was completed when Mom and I met with Kim and our book designer, Mercy Hope. As we met, it occurred to us that this day was also a one year anniversary. We met on June 10, 2015 and I had been released from rehab on June 10, 2014.

God knew my heart was to begin telling this story. What no one else knew is that secretly, Kim and I began meeting in the winter of my isolation. We took extreme germ prevention precautions. She commuted almost weekly to join me at Mom's place. We shared snacks and coffee.

We quickly discovered that God had been working behind the scenes to clear her calendar in a way that would make it possible for three months of writing and concept developing to take place as winter gave way to spring. Our meetings were full of faith, laughter and tears as the process of re-telling felt more like re-living for me and for Mom.

So there is my spring secret. I have been in my quiet place writing this story so at the appointed time, when Jesus says "Go," I will throw the door of this house open and emerge full of life and ready to tell anyone anywhere that my life feels a bit like an empty tomb. God has shown me that it is going to leave a lot of people searching for Jesus just as in the day of His empty tomb.

French author Albert Camus once wrote, *"In the depth of winter, I finally learned that within me there lay an invincible summer."* I can almost feel the long winter giving way to the hope of summer and new life.

I just received the good news that my house arrest will

lift at the end of April. My first act of faith was to book that promised and anticipated trip to the beach. I will head to the Atlantic while Kim heads to the Pacific. Separately, we will walk in the sand, splash in the waves and wonder what just hit us as this book goes to print.

One day toward the end of my house arrest while working on the manuscript, I had to block out construction noise. The same friends who had labored to build a wheelchair ramp that allowed me to get into Mom's home were here dismantling it, as I was now able to ascend and descend the small couple of steps. I took a break from my writing to simply listen. The sound impacted my heart in an unexpected way. It later occurred to me that the sound of hammers and saws represented these past painful months being dismantled piece by piece.

It is my deepest heart's desire for every person to find some piece of encouragement from my story. I can almost picture each of you leaning in to capture the personal sounds that represent the pain of your past being torn down to make way for a new season.

A season I anticipated to be lonely and dark became the season that produced the book you now hold in your hands. Actually, it was dark and lonely at times but if you could ask any seed buried in the cold dirt, it would likely say it began in a dark and lonely place. But it doesn't stay there. It begins to germinate and sprout, eventually pushing its way out of the dark as it springs up toward the sun.

Jesus taught a great deal in the Word about seed. Here are just a few examples where He speaks:

"This is the Lords declaration. 'For as heaven is higher than earth, so My ways are higher than your ways, and My thoughts than your thoughts. For just as rain and snow fall from heaven and do not return there without saturating the earth and making it germinate and sprout, and providing seed to sow and food to eat, so My word that comes from My mouth will not return to Me empty, but it will accomplish what I please and will prosper in what I send it to do.'" Isaiah 55: 8b-11

"I tell you the truth, unless a kernel of wheat is planted in the soil and dies, it remains alone. But its death will produce many new kernels – a plentiful harvest of new lives." John 12:24 NLT

"The One who sows good seed is the Son of Man." Matt 13:37

As you read my story, I wish I could hear about the details of this season of your life. Since we may never have a chance to talk over coffee and red velvet Oreos, I want to leave you with the assurance that has taken hold of my heart and now anchors my days to Jesus and His highest plan for my life.

I now know that the most extreme darkness marks the start of a new day. Think of your own clock. Midnight begins the a.m. shift while darkness is still pervasive, and yet it is the start of a new day.

I now know that when it feels you have just gone into a cocoon of death, a new species is about to emerge that possesses the ability to fly, not crawl. Just consider the caterpillar and the butterfly.

I now know that the written Word of God and the spoken prophetic words of life that emerge as the saints pray, will never return void but will bring a harvest full of life.

I now know that God is anxiously waiting for us to give Him our entire lives so that He can prosper and perfect His ultimate destinies in us and through us. Only then will a dying world be reconciled to Him.

I now know that if I live my life unto my own plans, it will remain solitary and small. But if I surrender my life to Jesus, He will build more than I could have ever imagined.

I now know that no matter what you or I ever walk through, the story is not finished.

I now know that God's Got This!

LAUREN SUMMEY SMITH has become a source of inspiration and determination to many.

As 2014 began, Lauren was enjoying life. By January 14th, she was fighting for her life. In the blink of an eye, H1N1 flu triggered a series of medical complications which almost ended her life.

While medical staff prepared for the possibility of death, her family, friends and a special doctor chose the path of faith. That is when miracles began to eclipse the darkness. Lauren emerged from this Tunnel of Change as a survivor who now waves the banner of hope with every fragile breath.

Lauren's hardest days awakened her true destiny. She now spends her days making public appearances, speaking and sharing her amazing survival story to challenge every person to value each breath, take hold of the life-line of faith in Jesus and live each day to its fullest.

She calls North Carolina home and finds the coast to be her greatest place of restoration.

Contact Lauren directly to discuss her availability for speaking appearances and to receive additional copies of God's Got This!

Email: Godsgotthis01@gmail.com
Web: creativelifenavigation.com
Phone: 828 228 5135 (talk/text)

KIM FLETCHER has awakened destinies and success strategies around the globe. She loves unlocking identity, vision and calling while elevating leadership and communication skills for clients including families, teams, staffs, ministries, companies and organizations.

Her skills as a Professional Life and Business Coach, Speaker/Trainer and four-time Author were honed in over thirty years spent serving as a Physical Therapist, Disability Advocate and College Instructor.

Kim spends her days sharing strategies that allowed her to launch her own life of freedom and impact.

Much like a seasoned sailor might use a compass to navigate, Kim brings direction that aligns individuals and groups with their highest impact and desired outcomes.

Contact Kim directly to consider a partnership for:

- One on one strategic Life or Business Coaching (by phone or face to face)

- Speaking or Training to upgrade the culture of your group or organization

- Co-authoring a book or article to share your unique story of impact

Email: kimfletchercoach@aol.com
Web: creativelifenavigation.com
Phone: 828 327 6702 (talk/text)

47383040R00145

Made in the USA
Charleston, SC
06 October 2015